JUMBLE®
MARATHON

Puzzles That Go the Distance!

T0192970

Henri Arnold
and
Bob Lee

TRIUMPH
BOOKS

Jumble® is a registered trademark
of Tribune Media Services, Inc.

Copyright © 2014 by Tribune Media Services, Inc.
All rights reserved.

This book is available in quantity at special discounts
for your group or organization.

For further information, contact:

Triumph Books LLC
814 North Franklin Street
Chicago, Illinois 60610
Phone: (312) 337-0747
www.triumphbooks.com

Printed in U.S.A.

ISBN: 978-1-60078-944-1

Design by Sue Knopf

CONTENTS

JUMBLE®

MARATHON

Classic Puzzles

PUZZLE 1

JUMBLE®

Unscramble these four Jumbles, one letter to each square, to form four ordinary words.

URPPE

LONBE

NASTEF

PHORTY

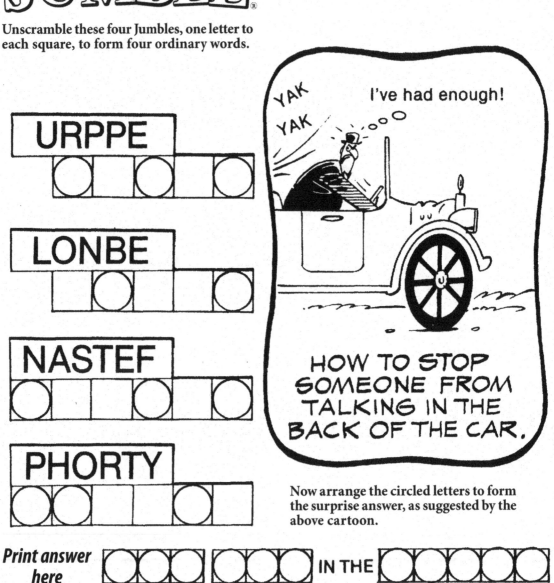

YAK
YAK
I've had enough!
HOW TO STOP SOMEONE FROM TALKING IN THE BACK OF THE CAR.

Now arrange the circled letters to form the surprise answer, as suggested by the above cartoon.

Print answer here ☐☐☐ ☐☐☐ IN THE ☐☐☐☐☐

PUZZLE 2

JUMBLE®

Unscramble these four Jumbles, one letter to each square, to form four ordinary words.

BRUTS

KLIMY

IPSOME

DESAUB

I always say honesty is the best policy
YOU CAN PROVE YOUR UPRIGHTNESS BY TAKING THIS LINE.

Now arrange the circled letters to form the surprise answer, as suggested by the above cartoon.

Print answer here

PUZZLE 3

JUMBLE®

Unscramble these four Jumbles, one letter to each square, to form four ordinary words.

RAPEP

BLEAC

CINFAG

DALINS

IT'S NOT COMPLETELY A "COLLAPSE"— JUST THIS.

Now arrange the circled letters to form the surprise answer, as suggested by the above cartoon.

Print answer here " "

PUZZLE 4

JUMBLE®

Unscramble these four Jumbles, one letter to each square, to form four ordinary words.

UMPEL

BALFE

DOOHKE

TALCOE

COMES UNDER PRESSURE WHEN A DRIVER STEPS ON IT.

Now arrange the circled letters to form the surprise answer, as suggested by the above cartoon.

Print answer here

PUZZLE 5

JUMBLE®

Unscramble these four Jumbles, one letter to each square, to form four ordinary words.

WECIT

CNOTH

DIRAHS

THOOSE

HOW FAR AWAY DID DAVID STAND FROM GOLIATH?

Now arrange the circled letters to form the surprise answer, as suggested by the above cartoon.

Print answer here A _ _ _ _ _ ' _ _ _ _ _ _ _

PUZZLE 6

JUMBLE®

Unscramble these four Jumbles, one letter to each square, to form four ordinary words.

RYTUL

BYGAG

NAWSER

WETSOB

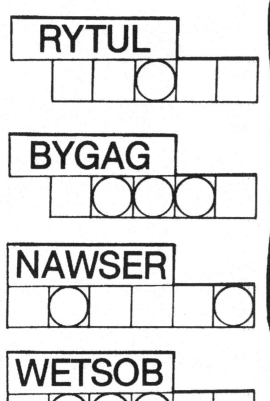

GIRLS
DANCE
DISCO
HOW THOSE ARTILLERYMEN WERE GOING.

Now arrange the circled letters to form the surprise answer, as suggested by the above cartoon.

Print answer here " "

PUZZLE 7

JUMBLE®

Unscramble these four Jumbles, one letter to each square, to form four ordinary words.

RAYRA

EPPIR

ENSCOD

HELSUB

WHAT SHE SAID BAKING A GOOD DESSERT WAS.

Now arrange the circled letters to form the surprise answer, as suggested by the above cartoon.

Print answer here

PUZZLE 8

JUMBLE®

Unscramble these four Jumbles, one letter to each square, to form four ordinary words.

NOJAB

CLECY

HARSHT

CEEDIT

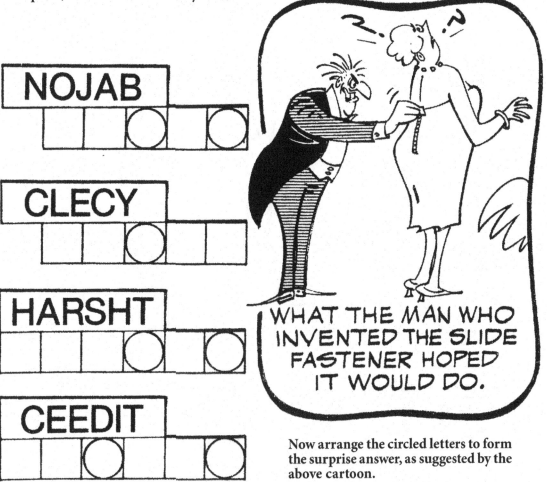

WHAT THE MAN WHO INVENTED THE SLIDE FASTENER HOPED IT WOULD DO.

Now arrange the circled letters to form the surprise answer, as suggested by the above cartoon.

Print answer here “ ”

PUZZLE 9

JUMBLE®

Unscramble these four Jumbles, one letter to each square, to form four ordinary words.

INEEC

BIELL

GORUBE

HERTAH

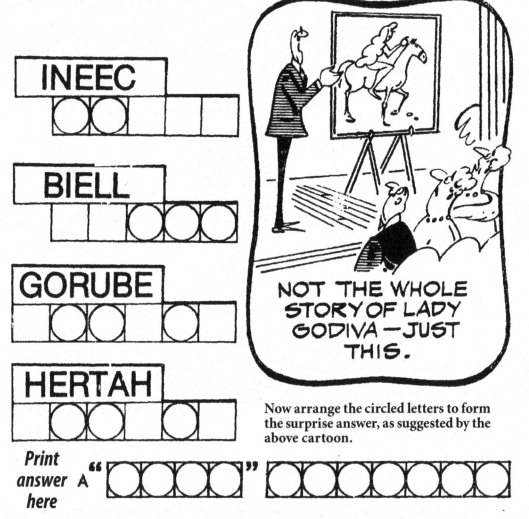

NOT THE WHOLE STORY OF LADY GODIVA—JUST THIS.

Now arrange the circled letters to form the surprise answer, as suggested by the above cartoon.

Print answer here A " "

PUZZLE 10

JUMBLE®

Unscramble these four Jumbles, one letter to each square, to form four ordinary words.

WORNC

SQUET

DRAFTI

FRYLUR

It'll sell a million records
WHAT TUNE MAKES A PERFORMER HAPPY?

Now arrange the circled letters to form the surprise answer, as suggested by the above cartoon.

Print answer here A "___-_____"

PUZZLE
11

JUMBLE®

Unscramble these four Jumbles, one letter to each square, to form four ordinary words.

CYREM

EVERF

TOZALE

GLABEM

It's easy
WHAT SAILING A BOAT MIGHT BE FOR AN EXPERIENCED SAILOR.

Now arrange the circled letters to form the surprise answer, as suggested by the above cartoon.

Print answer here A " "

PUZZLE 12

JUMBLE®

Unscramble these four Jumbles, one letter to each square, to form four ordinary words.

HOPNY

YURMM

UNMAUT

NAFELL

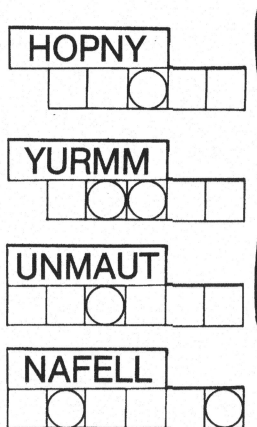

WIN
PLACE
ON WHICH HE PLACED MONEY OF A CERTAIN AMOUNT.

Now arrange the circled letters to form the surprise answer, as suggested by the above cartoon.

Print answer here

PUZZLE 13

JUMBLE®

Unscramble these four Jumbles, one letter to each square, to form four ordinary words.

MILOB

DAAMM

BUHSIL

PIMAGE

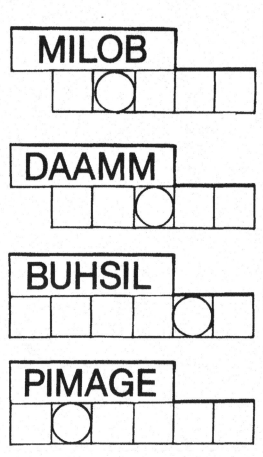

WHERE IT COULD BE SAID AT A BANQUET.

Now arrange the circled letters to form the surprise answer, as suggested by the above cartoon.

Print answer here THE " "

PUZZLE 14

JUMBLE®

Unscramble these four Jumbles, one letter to each square, to form four ordinary words.

PRUSN

HOPUC

ROTRAM

HISVAL

COULD THEY BE CHISELERS EMPLOYED ON "RELIEF" PROJECTS?

Now arrange the circled letters to form the surprise answer, as suggested by the above cartoon.

Print answer here

PUZZLE 15

JUMBLE®

Unscramble these four Jumbles, one letter to each square, to form four ordinary words.

TADAP

LEWJE

TRAULB

NACAMI

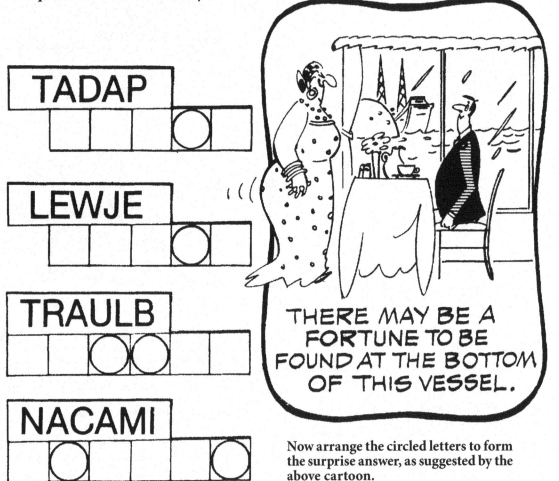

THERE MAY BE A FORTUNE TO BE FOUND AT THE BOTTOM OF THIS VESSEL.

Now arrange the circled letters to form the surprise answer, as suggested by the above cartoon.

Print answer here A

PUZZLE 16

JUMBLE®

Unscramble these four Jumbles, one letter to each square, to form four ordinary words.

MYPTE

RIVOS

PENOLL

LYNFOD

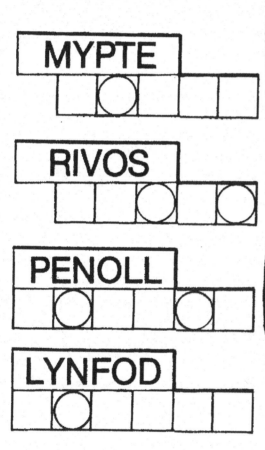

WHAT OVER-
EATING MAKES
THE TORSO.

Now arrange the circled letters to form the surprise answer, as suggested by the above cartoon.

Print answer here “ ”

PUZZLE
17

JUMBLE®

Unscramble these four Jumbles, one letter to each square, to form four ordinary words.

NAHDY

LOMOB

NAITED

EWSUIN

HOW JONAH FELT WHEN THE WHALE SWALLOWED HIM.

Now arrange the circled letters to form the surprise answer, as suggested by the above cartoon.

Print answer here ◯◯◯◯ – IN – THE – ◯◯◯◯◯

PUZZLE 18

JUMBLE®

Unscramble these four Jumbles, one letter to each square, to form four ordinary words.

SIGEE

RUSIV

POTTIE

REDOBT

Haven't a thing to wear
$
WHAT SOME WOMEN CLAIM TO BE.

Now arrange the circled letters to form the surprise answer, as suggested by the above cartoon.

Print answer here " "

PUZZLE 19

JUMBLE®

Unscramble these four Jumbles, one letter to each square, to form four ordinary words.

RYPEK

SINBO

YAUNES

KALTEC

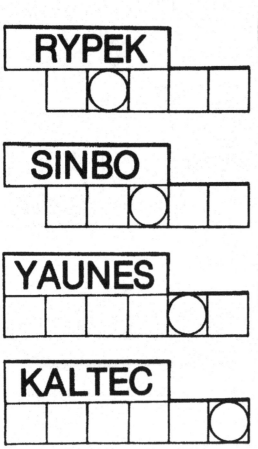

LOOKS AT THEM COMING AND GOING — IN BOTH DIRECTIONS.

Now arrange the circled letters to form the surprise answer, as suggested by the above cartoon.

Print answer here

PUZZLE 20

JUMBLE®

Unscramble these four Jumbles, one letter to each square, to form four ordinary words.

WONIG

HILEW

RALOPP

LESCUM

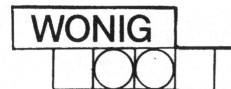

For the old man
Shhh
THE GENERAL'S FAVORITE HEADQUARTERS.

Now arrange the circled letters to form the surprise answer, as suggested by the above cartoon.

Print answer here

PUZZLE 21

JUMBLE®

Unscramble these four Jumbles, one letter to each square, to form four ordinary words.

INGGO

KLUFE

FLABEL

CLARRO

Breakfast, dear?
WHAT VAMPIRES OFTEN TAKE AT MIDNIGHT.

Now arrange the circled letters to form the surprise answer, as suggested by the above cartoon.

Print answer here A

PUZZLE 22

JUMBLE®

Unscramble these four Jumbles, one letter to each square, to form four ordinary words.

NOVEM

YURRC

PRAUPE

ENFLOY

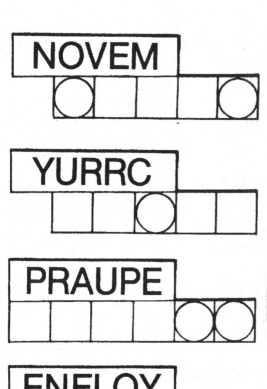

?!
HOW TO MAKE VARNISH DISAPPEAR.

Now arrange the circled letters to form the surprise answer, as suggested by the above cartoon.

Print answer here THE

JUMBLE®

Unscramble these four Jumbles, one letter to each square, to form four ordinary words.

TOIDI

DEWEG

RORTER

COLUSH

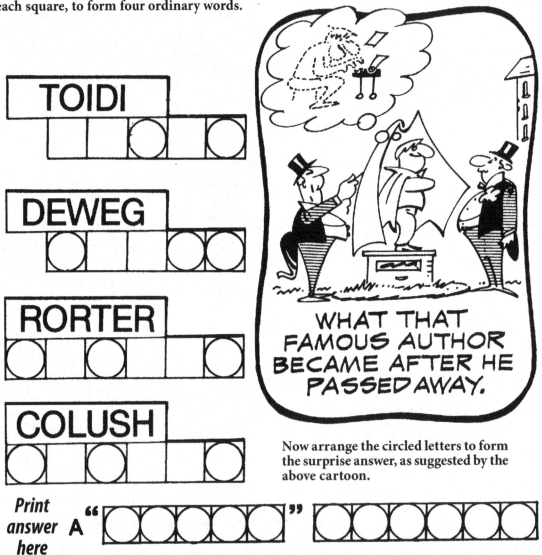

WHAT THAT FAMOUS AUTHOR BECAME AFTER HE PASSED AWAY.

Now arrange the circled letters to form the surprise answer, as suggested by the above cartoon.

Print answer here A " "

PUZZLE 24

JUMBLE®

Unscramble these four Jumbles, one letter to each square, to form four ordinary words.

USSOE

LUCCK

JUDSAT

INTOOL

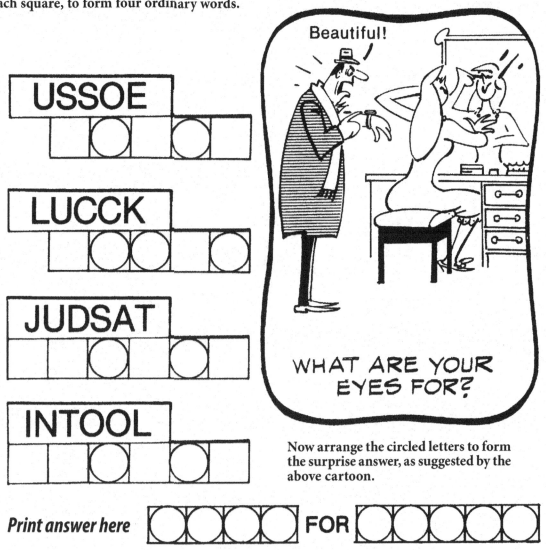

Beautiful!
WHAT ARE YOUR EYES FOR?

Now arrange the circled letters to form the surprise answer, as suggested by the above cartoon.

Print answer here ◯◯◯◯ FOR ◯◯◯◯◯

PUZZLE 25

JUMBLE®

Unscramble these four Jumbles, one letter to each square, to form four ordinary words.

VEYHA

RITHM

HYNTAS

MORNED

WHAT HAPPENED TO LADY GODIVA'S HORSE WHEN HE SAW SHE HAD NO CLOTHES ON?

Now arrange the circled letters to form the surprise answer, as suggested by the above cartoon.

Print answer here IT " "

JUMBLE®

MARATHON

Daily Puzzles

PUZZLE 26

JUMBLE®

Unscramble these four Jumbles, one letter to each square, to form four ordinary words.

YOPPP

HOBAR

KENASH

RAWLEY

THE HANGMAN'S FAVORITE READING MATERIAL.

Now arrange the circled letters to form the surprise answer, as suggested by the above cartoon.

Print answer here A "◯◯◯◯◯◯◯◯◯◯"

PUZZLE 27

JUMBLE®

Unscramble these four Jumbles, one letter to each square, to form four ordinary words.

CRAHN

PLIME

MEESID

INGELT

Nice promotion

WHAT THE GHOST WHO JOINED THE POLICE FORCE BECAME.

Now arrange the circled letters to form the surprise answer, as suggested by the above cartoon.

Print answer here _ _ – " _ _ _ _ _ _ _ "

PUZZLE 28

JUMBLE®

Unscramble these four Jumbles, one letter to each square, to form four ordinary words.

TIFFY

NASPY

RAAPPE

PLOARE

You're all going on a long journey
WHAT YOU MIGHT GET FROM PIRATES.

Now arrange the circled letters to form the surprise answer, as suggested by the above cartoon.

Print answer here A "◯◯◯ ◯◯◯◯◯"

PUZZLE 29

JUMBLE®

Unscramble these four Jumbles, one letter to each square, to form four ordinary words.

MUTON

KNAWE

TEASTE

ACLOSE

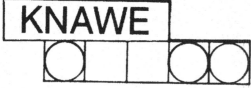

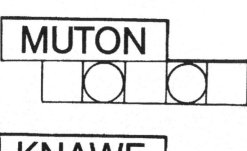

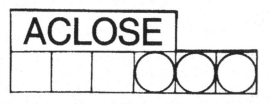

Sorry . . .
M.D.
WHAT THE VERY BUSY DOCTOR SAID TO THE INVISIBLE MAN.

Now arrange the circled letters to form the surprise answer, as suggested by the above cartoon.

Print answer here ___ _ ____ YOU ___

PUZZLE 30

JUMBLE®

Unscramble these four Jumbles, one letter to each square, to form four ordinary words.

GAMLE

JEGUD

BASHUM

DAGAPO

WHY IT WAS SO HARD TO REMOVE THE COVER FROM THE MARMALADE JAR.

Now arrange the circled letters to form the surprise answer, as suggested by the above cartoon.

Print answer here IT WAS " "

PUZZLE 31

JUMBLE®

Unscramble these four Jumbles, one letter to each square, to form four ordinary words.

HIFAT

PLYSH

FAISAR

SPITTY

WHY THE JUDGE GAVE THE MAN WHO STOLE SOME LINGERIE A SUS-PENDED SENTENCE.

Now arrange the circled letters to form the surprise answer, as suggested by the above cartoon.

Print answer here IT WAS

PUZZLE 32

JUMBLE®

Unscramble these four Jumbles, one letter to each square, to form four ordinary words.

PRUTE

MOCEA

BUCHER

BIMGAT

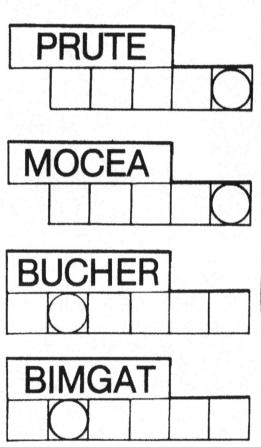

A FOUR-LETTER SWEAR WORD OFTEN HEARD IN LEGAL CIRCLES.

Now arrange the circled letters to form the surprise answer, as suggested by the above cartoon.

Print answer here " "

PUZZLE 33

JUMBLE®

Unscramble these four Jumbles, one letter to each square, to form four ordinary words.

YAHNE

CABIS

REDAIM

TRYGEN

HE FELT LIKE THIS AFTER HIS LAUNDRY FINALLY CAME BACK.

Now arrange the circled letters to form the surprise answer, as suggested by the above cartoon.

Print answer here A

PUZZLE 34

JUMBLE®

Unscramble these four Jumbles, one letter to each square, to form four ordinary words.

KORPE

TILMI

COLKUN

ERPICH

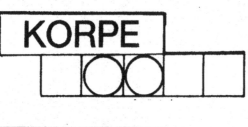

I wanna be just like him when I grow up

WHAT MOST PEOPLE DO WHEN THEY MEET THAT FAMOUS BASKETBALL STAR.

Now arrange the circled letters to form the surprise answer, as suggested by the above cartoon.

Print answer here ◯◯◯◯ ◯'◯ TO ◯◯◯

PUZZLE 35

JUMBLE®

Unscramble these four Jumbles, one letter to each square, to form four ordinary words.

LIVAL

UNPER

INREET

LISGRY

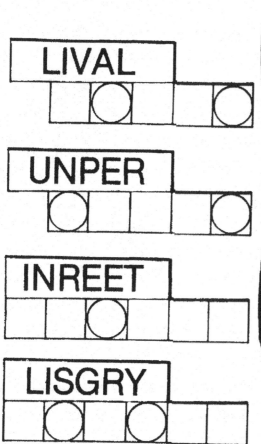

WHAT BAD SAILORS ARE CALLED.

Now arrange the circled letters to form the surprise answer, as suggested by the above cartoon.

Print answer here

PUZZLE 36

JUMBLE®

Unscramble these four Jumbles, one letter to each square, to form four ordinary words.

SACEE

NOFET

DEEBIS

HURGOT

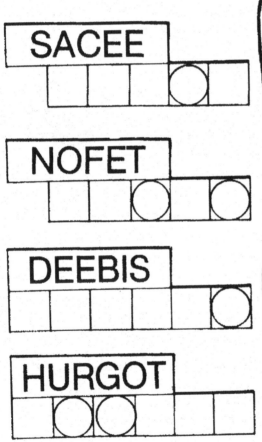

opera!
YOU MAY GET NO REST FROM THESE SINGERS.

Now arrange the circled letters to form the surprise answer, as suggested by the above cartoon.

Print answer here “ ”

PUZZLE 37

JUMBLE®

Unscramble these four Jumbles, one letter to each square, to form four ordinary words.

LIRLT

VELDE

CAEPIE

INLARM

Better be careful what I say!
WATCHES ONE'S WORDS.

Now arrange the circled letters to form the surprise answer, as suggested by the above cartoon.

Print answer here A ( ) ( ) ( ) - ( ) ( ) ( ) ( ) ( ) ( )

PUZZLE 38

JUMBLE®

Unscramble these four Jumbles, one letter to each square, to form four ordinary words.

ADGUY

ROVIY

MERPIT

INYELC

SALE ON REFERENCE BOOKS
HE DIDN'T KNOW THE MEANING OF FEAR UNTIL SOMEONE GAVE HIM THIS.

Now arrange the circled letters to form the surprise answer, as suggested by the above cartoon.

Print answer here A

PUZZLE 39

JUMBLE®

Unscramble these four Jumbles, one letter to each square, to form four ordinary words.

EMARK

BIASS

UPDELD

DOGOLY

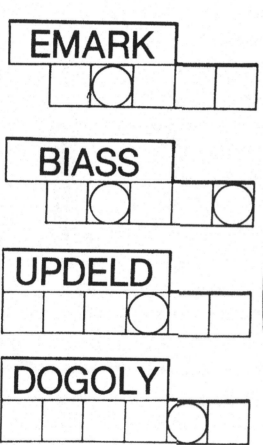

I'm starved!
IT'S OFTEN EATEN AFTER DRESSING.

Now arrange the circled letters to form the surprise answer, as suggested by the above cartoon.

Print answer here

PUZZLE 40

JUMBLE®

Unscramble these four Jumbles, one letter to each square, to form four ordinary words.

VALIA

OPSOW

DYKLIN

DRUSAB

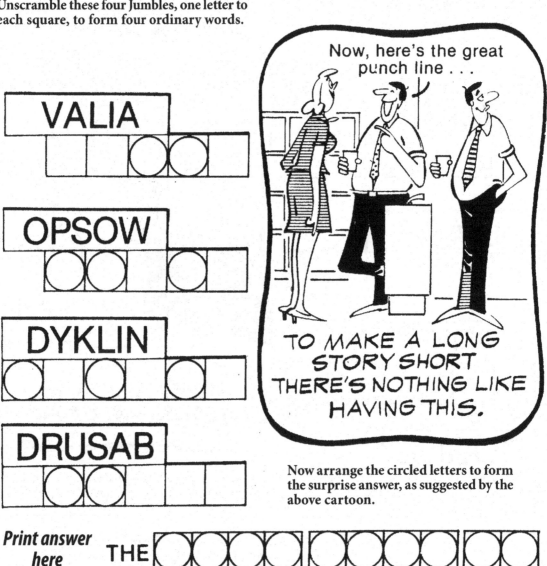

Now, here's the great punch line . . .
TO MAKE A LONG STORY SHORT THERE'S NOTHING LIKE HAVING THIS.

Now arrange the circled letters to form the surprise answer, as suggested by the above cartoon.

Print answer here THE

PUZZLE 41

JUMBLE®

Unscramble these four Jumbles, one letter to each square, to form four ordinary words.

TABOU

DISTA

DEMUGS

SENNIG

HOW HE SURVIVED THE SHIPWRECK.

Now arrange the circled letters to form the surprise answer, as suggested by the above cartoon.

Print answer here HE ______ THE ____

PUZZLE 42

JUMBLE®

Unscramble these four Jumbles, one letter to each square, to form four ordinary words.

GOMAD

RUMON

UNBOTT

TIDOAR

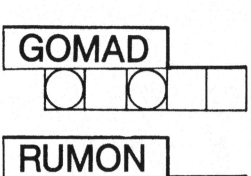

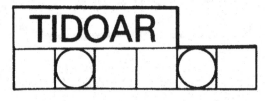

Our first date

FLOWERS MAY BE APPROPRIATE WHEN THE ROMANCE IS THIS.

Now arrange the circled letters to form the surprise answer, as suggested by the above cartoon.

Print answer here A "________" ONE

PUZZLE 43

JUMBLE®

Unscramble these four Jumbles, one letter to each square, to form four ordinary words.

RECSS

OATAR

TECKOP

MAYLIF

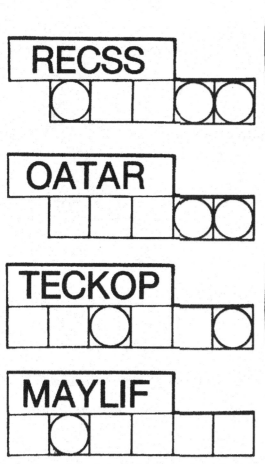

WHAT THOSE THINGS THAT HIT THE ACTORS WERE.

Now arrange the circled letters to form the surprise answer, as suggested by the above cartoon.

Print answer here ☐☐☐☐ AT THE ☐☐☐☐

PUZZLE 44

JUMBLE®

Unscramble these four Jumbles, one letter to each square, to form four ordinary words.

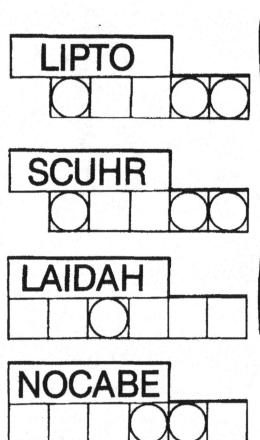

NO! Go out and play
A KIND OF SCOTCH SUITABLE FOR CHILDREN?!

LIPTO

SCUHR

LAIDAH

NOCABE

Now arrange the circled letters to form the surprise answer, as suggested by the above cartoon.

Print answer here

PUZZLE 45

JUMBLE®

Unscramble these four Jumbles, one letter to each square, to form four ordinary words.

GOGER

DEUXE

ZOLENZ

DROBIF

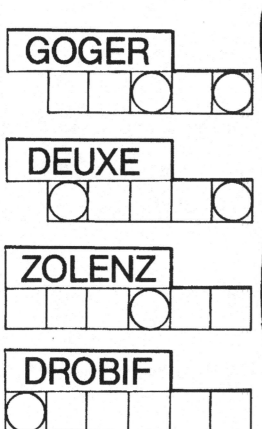

WHAT THE COP SAID TO THE BURGLAR.

Now arrange the circled letters to form the surprise answer, as suggested by the above cartoon.

Print answer here !

PUZZLE 46

JUMBLE®

Unscramble these four Jumbles, one letter to each square, to form four ordinary words.

TIMAY

HINSY

YUGLIT

KRALTE

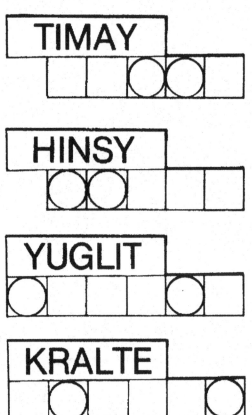

YOU WOULDN'T EXPECT THIS TO BE A CROOKED POKER HAND, WOULD YOU?

Now arrange the circled letters to form the surprise answer, as suggested by the above cartoon.

Print answer here A " "

PUZZLE 47

JUMBLE®

Unscramble these four Jumbles, one letter to each square, to form four ordinary words.

GUGOE

KAYLB

VEENAU

GELISH

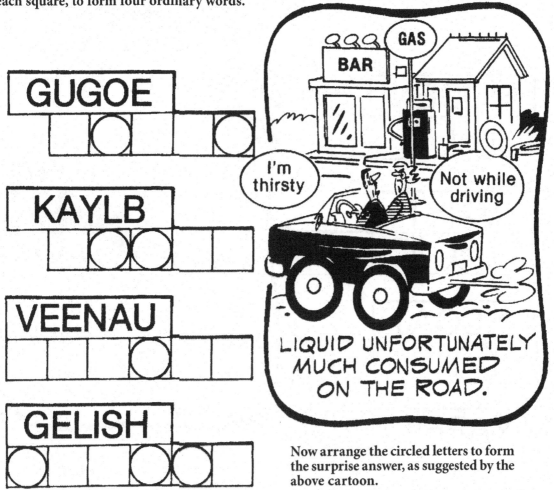

GAS
BAR
I'm thirsty
Not while driving
LIQUID UNFORTUNATELY MUCH CONSUMED ON THE ROAD.

Now arrange the circled letters to form the surprise answer, as suggested by the above cartoon.

Print answer here

PUZZLE 48

JUMBLE®

Unscramble these four Jumbles, one letter to each square, to form four ordinary words.

MODEN

VAIST

INDOAJ

YARFIL

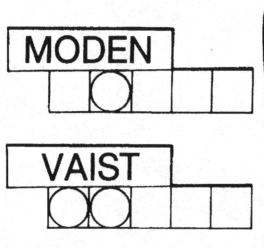

DIVE IN! IT CAN BE HEAVENLY

Now arrange the circled letters to form the surprise answer, as suggested by the above cartoon.

Print answer here " "

PUZZLE 49

JUMBLE®

Unscramble these four Jumbles, one letter to each square, to form four ordinary words.

CAMKS

ZYCAR

MERDIP

LOONED

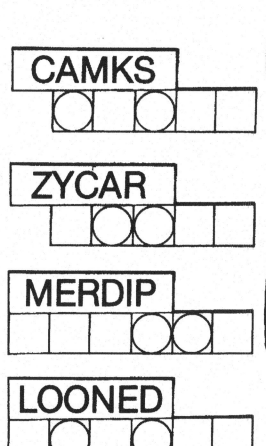

WHAT HAPPENED WHEN HE ACCIDENTLY PULLED THE ALTITUDE STICK?

Now arrange the circled letters to form the surprise answer, as suggested by the above cartoon.

Print answer here IT ☐☐☐☐ HIM "☐☐☐☐"

PUZZLE 50

JUMBLE®

Unscramble these four Jumbles, one letter to each square, to form four ordinary words.

TEENA

STURB

BEDFAL

STURME

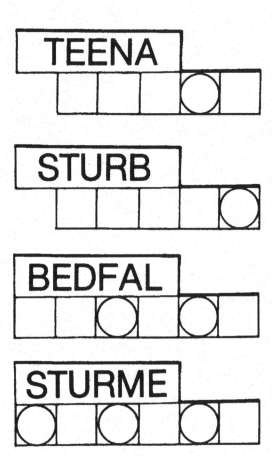

WHO RAIDED MY VEGETABLE PATCH?
3-8

Now arrange the circled letters to form the surprise answer, as suggested by the above cartoon.

Print answer here " "

PUZZLE
51

JUMBLE®

Unscramble these four Jumbles, one letter to each square, to form four ordinary words.

KAROC

FOOLI

LIEDEY

HINGKT

E=mc2
WHAT A PERSON WHO THINKS BY THE YARD AND DOES BY THE INCH MIGHT GET.

Now arrange the circled letters to form the surprise answer, as suggested by the above cartoon.

Print answer here ☐☐☐☐☐☐ BY THE ☐☐☐☐

PUZZLE 52

JUMBLE®

Unscramble these four Jumbles, one letter to each square, to form four ordinary words.

FLATA

TOBAB

INTADE

ENBATE

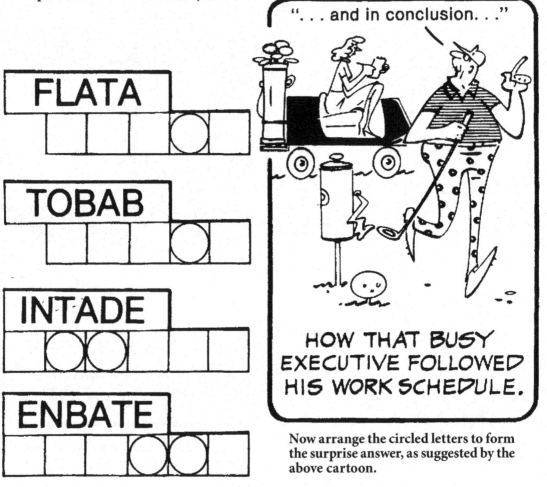

"... and in conclusion..."
HOW THAT BUSY EXECUTIVE FOLLOWED HIS WORK SCHEDULE.

Now arrange the circled letters to form the surprise answer, as suggested by the above cartoon.

Print answer here ◯◯◯ ◯ "◯◯◯"

PUZZLE
53

JUMBLE®

Unscramble these four Jumbles, one letter to each square, to form four ordinary words.

INYAR

HEWLS

RUJINO

LACKET

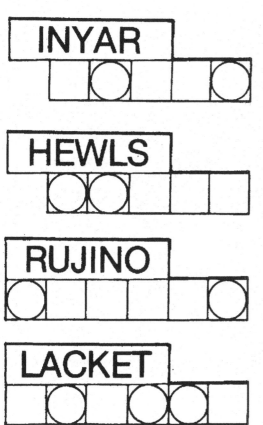

NEVER KNOWS WHERE HIS NEXT CAR IS COMING FROM.

Now arrange the circled letters to form the surprise answer, as suggested by the above cartoon.

Print answer here A

PUZZLE 54

JUMBLE®

Unscramble these four Jumbles, one letter to each square, to form four ordinary words.

RADAW

ZIPER

GREATY

CHOPON

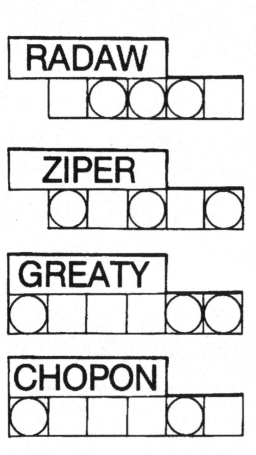

YOU CAN HELP KEEP THOSE FOOD BILLS DOWN WITH THIS.

Now arrange the circled letters to form the surprise answer, as suggested by the above cartoon.

Print answer here A

PUZZLE 55

JUMBLE®

Unscramble these four Jumbles, one letter to each square, to form four ordinary words.

WRONC

TUBIL

FLIDED

VERPOL

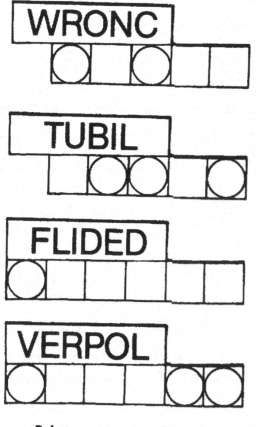

WHAT SHE GAVE HIM WHEN HE ASKED WHETHER HE COULD SEE HER HOME.

Now arrange the circled letters to form the surprise answer, as suggested by the above cartoon.

Print answer here A ○○○○○○○ ○○ IT

PUZZLE 56

JUMBLE®

Unscramble these four Jumbles, one letter to each square, to form four ordinary words.

BILLE

ASSOB

SOOJUY

NAITAT

JUST MARRIED
ALL SHE KNEW ABOUT COOKING WAS HOW TO BRING HER HUSBAND THIS.

Now arrange the circled letters to form the surprise answer, as suggested by the above cartoon.

Print answer here

PUZZLE 57

JUMBLE®

Unscramble these four Jumbles, one letter to each square, to form four ordinary words.

YACKT

NIFYN

SAWLAY

LEWOLF

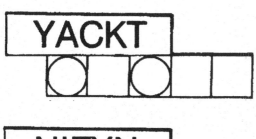

MR. JONES
MS. SMITH
SOME GOSSIPS WOULD RATHER LISTEN TO DIRT THAN DO THIS.

Now arrange the circled letters to form the surprise answer, as suggested by the above cartoon.

Print answer here

PUZZLE 58

JUMBLE®

Unscramble these four Jumbles, one letter to each square, to form four ordinary words.

MERIN

MARRE

ZAHDAR

BURPAT

PEOPLE WHO SING LIKE A CANARY SELDOM EAT LIKE THIS.

Now arrange the circled letters to form the surprise answer, as suggested by the above cartoon.

Print answer here

PUZZLE 59

JUMBLE®

Unscramble these four Jumbles, one letter to each square, to form four ordinary words.

YUMST

WARBL

YETHIG

GLIEGG

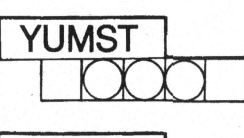

STATE LINE
P.D.
WHAT THEY CALLED THOSE CIGARETTE SMUGGLERS.

Now arrange the circled letters to form the surprise answer, as suggested by the above cartoon.

Print answer here " ____ - ________ "

PUZZLE 60

JUMBLE®

Unscramble these four Jumbles, one letter to each square, to form four ordinary words.

GINVY

CUHDY

LEHTAH

TUFACE

WHAT THOSE FELINE GOSSIPS WERE.

Now arrange the circled letters to form the surprise answer, as suggested by the above cartoon.

Print answer here " "

PUZZLE 61

JUMBLE®

Unscramble these four Jumbles, one letter to each square, to form four ordinary words.

REXET

TASEC

YUTPED

BINBBO

WHEN IT COMES TO VACATIONS, A GIRL CAN GO TO THE MOUNTAINS AND SEE THE SCENERY, OR GO TO THE BEACH AND DO THIS.

Now arrange the circled letters to form the surprise answer, as suggested by the above cartoon.

Print answer here ◯◯ THE ◯◯◯◯◯◯◯

PUZZLE 62

JUMBLE®

Unscramble these four Jumbles, one letter to each square, to form four ordinary words.

HEMIC

RUYLS

MAULSY

TIBBEG

He'll be sorry
WHAT IGNORANCE AT THE BEACH COULD BE.

Now arrange the circled letters to form the surprise answer, as suggested by the above cartoon.

Print answer here "_ _ _ _ _ - _ _ _"

PUZZLE 63

JUMBLE®

Unscramble these four Jumbles, one letter to each square, to form four ordinary words.

DEALL

VENAK

CAJEKT

THUSIA

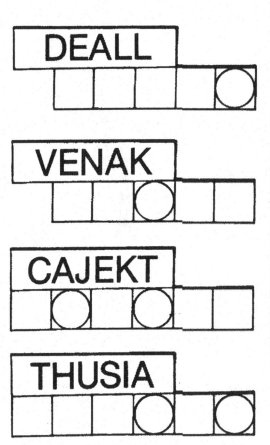

WHAT A THOUGHTFUL WIFE HAS READY WHEN HER HUSBAND COMES HOME FROM A FISHING TRIP.

Now arrange the circled letters to form the surprise answer, as suggested by the above cartoon.

Print answer here

PUZZLE 64

JUMBLE®

Unscramble these four Jumbles, one letter to each square, to form four ordinary words.

WYLLO

NILAF

DARFOE

NATTEX

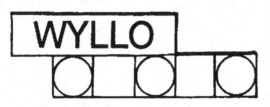

WHEN THIS HAPPENED, THAT COMEDIAN HELD HIS AUDIENCE OPEN-MOUTHED.

Now arrange the circled letters to form the surprise answer, as suggested by the above cartoon.

Print answer here THEY

PUZZLE 65

JUMBLE®

Unscramble these four Jumbles, one letter to each square, to form four ordinary words.

FRADT

MERIG

FRINEY

GIZAHN

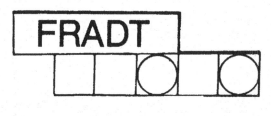

A GUY WHO CLAIMS HE'S ALWAYS THIS MUST BE ALL WET.

Now arrange the circled letters to form the surprise answer, as suggested by the above cartoon.

Print answer here ☐☐☐☐☐ AS ☐☐☐☐

PUZZLE 66

JUMBLE®

Unscramble these four Jumbles, one letter to each square, to form four ordinary words.

OUSLE

USHOE

BACHEL

ROTGOT

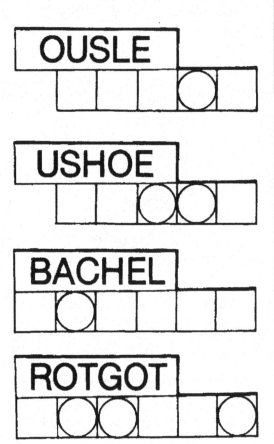

WHAT A GUY WHO'S NEVER AT A LOSS FOR WORDS OFTEN IS.

Now arrange the circled letters to form the surprise answer, as suggested by the above cartoon.

Print answer here

PUZZLE 67

JUMBLE®

Unscramble these four Jumbles, one letter to each square, to form four ordinary words.

LYKIM

ZOONE

HYCTOU

GROITE

WHAT A HUSBAND MISSES WHEN HIS WIFE ISN'T.

Now arrange the circled letters to form the surprise answer, as suggested by the above cartoon.

Print answer here

PUZZLE 68

JUMBLE®

Unscramble these four Jumbles, one letter to each square, to form four ordinary words.

NOWVE

BIATH

EEDDAC

HASFIM

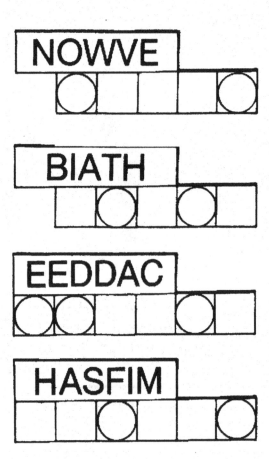

HOW THE FARMER KNEW IT WAS TIME TO GET UP.

Now arrange the circled letters to form the surprise answer, as suggested by the above cartoon.

Print answer here IT ◯◯◯◯◯◯ ON ◯◯◯

PUZZLE 69

JUMBLE®

Unscramble these four Jumbles, one letter to each square, to form four ordinary words.

IGSEE

RAJOM

UNNACE

BALGER

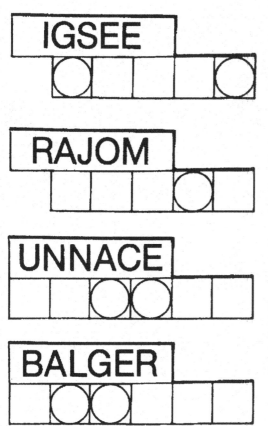

WHEN A MAN BRINGS HIS WIFE FLOWERS "FOR NO REASON AT ALL," THERE'S USUALLY THIS.

Now arrange the circled letters to form the surprise answer, as suggested by the above cartoon.

Print answer here

PUZZLE 70

JUMBLE®

Unscramble these four Jumbles, one letter to each square, to form four ordinary words.

MURYM

DRUFA

FICTEN

GLOONB

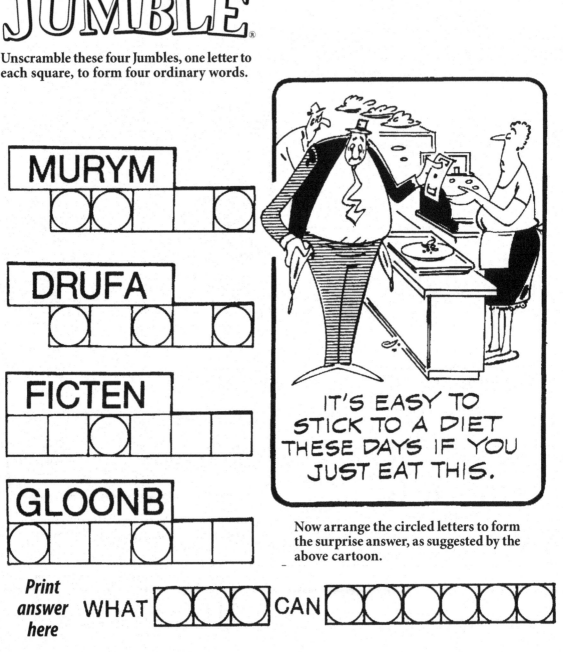

IT'S EASY TO STICK TO A DIET THESE DAYS IF YOU JUST EAT THIS.

Now arrange the circled letters to form the surprise answer, as suggested by the above cartoon.

Print answer here WHAT ☐☐☐ CAN ☐☐☐☐☐☐

PUZZLE 71

JUMBLE®

Unscramble these four Jumbles, one letter to each square, to form four ordinary words.

CUHLG

TRIGE

THRIME

UPDINT

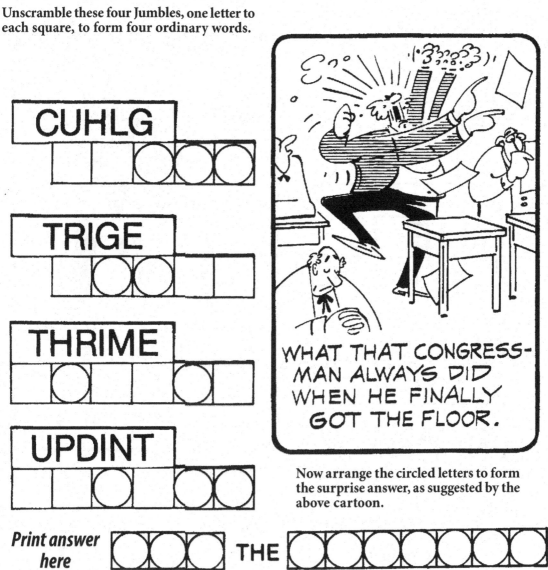

WHAT THAT CONGRESS-MAN ALWAYS DID WHEN HE FINALLY GOT THE FLOOR.

Now arrange the circled letters to form the surprise answer, as suggested by the above cartoon.

Print answer here ◯◯◯ THE ◯◯◯◯◯◯◯

PUZZLE 72

JUMBLE®

Unscramble these four Jumbles, one letter to each square, to form four ordinary words.

MANUH

HILTE

TALMEL

GINGON

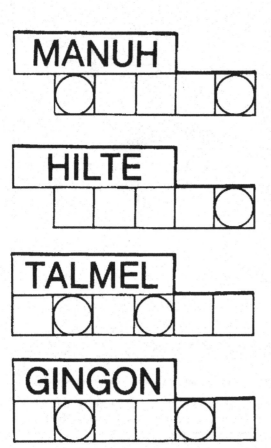

They're raising the fares again
TRAINS
NO MATTER HOW CONDITIONS IMPROVE IN THAT BIG CITY, THE SUBWAY ALWAYS APPEARS TO BE THIS.

Now arrange the circled letters to form the surprise answer, as suggested by the above cartoon.

Print answer here " ◯◯ ◯ ◯◯◯◯ "

PUZZLE 73

JUMBLE®

Unscramble these four Jumbles, one letter to each square, to form four ordinary words.

KANLY

CAXTE

REJESY

RIMPIA

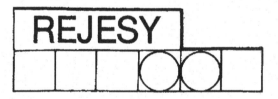

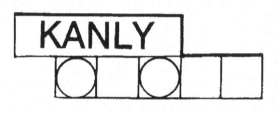

WHAT THE CIRCUS STRONG MAN TURNED CROOK HAD TO BE.

Now arrange the circled letters to form the surprise answer, as suggested by the above cartoon.

Print answer here A ◯◯◯ OF "◯◯◯◯◯"

PUZZLE 74

JUMBLE®

Unscramble these four Jumbles, one letter to each square, to form four ordinary words.

NEKEL

TACCH

BOADUN

BODLIE

HOW A BARBER USUALLY LIKES TO TALK.

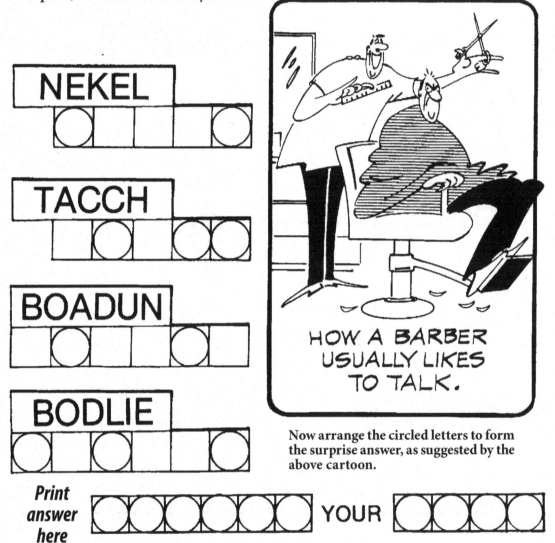

Now arrange the circled letters to form the surprise answer, as suggested by the above cartoon.

Print answer here ______ YOUR ____

PUZZLE 75

JUMBLE®

Unscramble these four Jumbles, one letter to each square, to form four ordinary words.

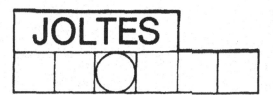

So Jackie O . . .
Then Lady Di . . .
Here are the inside facts . . .

WHAT THOSE GOSSIP REPORTERS OFTEN GIVE YOU THE LOWDOWN ON.

ULIPP

ARVEG

JOLTES

THRAHE

Now arrange the circled letters to form the surprise answer, as suggested by the above cartoon.

Print answer here THE ______-___

PUZZLE
76

JUMBLE®

Unscramble these four Jumbles, one letter to each square, to form four ordinary words.

TOODU

RAYAR

PRUSHE

CREBIK

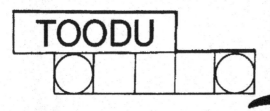

WHEN YOU SAVE MONEY FOR A RAINY DAY, SOME-ONE ALWAYS COMES ALONG AT THE LAST MINUTE TO DO THIS.

Now arrange the circled letters to form the surprise answer, as suggested by the above cartoon.

Print answer here

PUZZLE 77

JUMBLE®

Unscramble these four Jumbles, one letter to each square, to form four ordinary words.

She told me to come here
HELP WANTED
HE JOINED THE FIRE DEPARTMENT BECAUSE SHE SAID THIS TO HIM.

LUGAH

ITUSE

HOCORB

ZILZES

Now arrange the circled letters to form the surprise answer, as suggested by the above cartoon.

Print answer here

PUZZLE 78

JUMBLE®

Unscramble these four Jumbles, one letter to each square, to form four ordinary words.

CILLA

MORRA

GLIJEN

DUIMBE

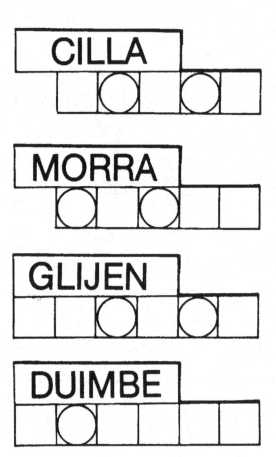

WHAT THEY CALL THAT MAN FROM WHOM MANY DIFFERENT GIRLS GET LOVE LETTERS.

Now arrange the circled letters to form the surprise answer, as suggested by the above cartoon.

Print answer here **THE**

PUZZLE 79

JUMBLE®

Unscramble these four Jumbles, one letter to each square, to form four ordinary words.

ROUCI

GREBA

KANNIP

RUMATE

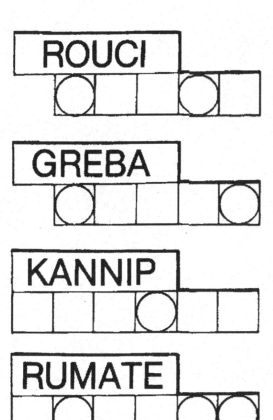

Glad to make your acquaintance
WHAT SOME SKATERS MIGHT HAVE TO DO IN ORDER TO GET BETTER ACQUAINTED.

Now arrange the circled letters to form the surprise answer, as suggested by the above cartoon.

Print answer here ☐☐☐☐☐ THE ☐☐☐

PUZZLE 80

JUMBLE®

Unscramble these four Jumbles, one letter to each square, to form four ordinary words.

RALNS

MARDA

CASSEC

VAHDLE

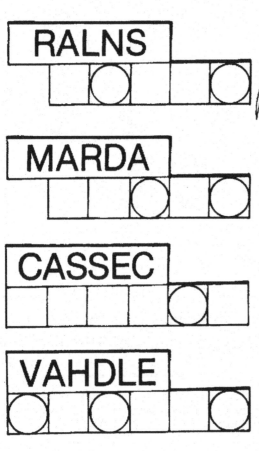

Let's take a rest
WHAT THE GUY WHO WAS "ALL FEET" WHEN HE DANCED WAS WHEN THEY SAT DOWN.

Now arrange the circled letters to form the surprise answer, as suggested by the above cartoon.

Print answer here

PUZZLE
81

JUMBLE®

Unscramble these four Jumbles, one letter to each square, to form four ordinary words.

REDOO

MIDIO

BYRBAC

RUINJY

HE DECIDED TO WATCH HIS DRINKING— BY ONLY VISITING BARS THAT HAVE THIS.

Now arrange the circled letters to form the surprise answer, as suggested by the above cartoon.

Print answer here A

PUZZLE 82

JUMBLE®

Unscramble these four Jumbles, one letter to each square, to form four ordinary words.

VALEE

ROPIR

ENGOPS

LYROOP

IF YOU THINK GOLF IS ONLY A RICH MAN'S GAME, LOOK AT THESE.

Now arrange the circled letters to form the surprise answer, as suggested by the above cartoon.

Print answer here ALL THE

PUZZLE 83

JUMBLE®

Unscramble these four Jumbles, one letter to each square, to form four ordinary words.

DOLOB

NOUGY

REWAYL

TEVVLE

What do you suggest?
WHAT HIS CURLY HAIR WAS BEGINNING TO DO.

Now arrange the circled letters to form the surprise answer, as suggested by the above cartoon.

Print answer here

PUZZLE 84

JUMBLE®

Unscramble these four Jumbles, one letter to each square, to form four ordinary words.

CANYF

ANUDT

INREEM

CEERUD

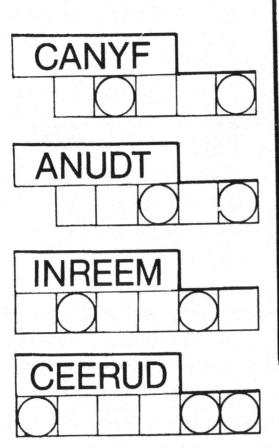

HE GOT THE JOB AS A PIANO MOVER ALTHOUGH HE COULDN'T EVEN DO THIS.

Now arrange the circled letters to form the surprise answer, as suggested by the above cartoon.

Print answer here ◯◯◯◯◯ A ◯◯◯◯

PUZZLE 85

JUMBLE®

Unscramble these four Jumbles, one letter to each square, to form four ordinary words.

AMFER

SIVOR

UNCOOP

GERUDD

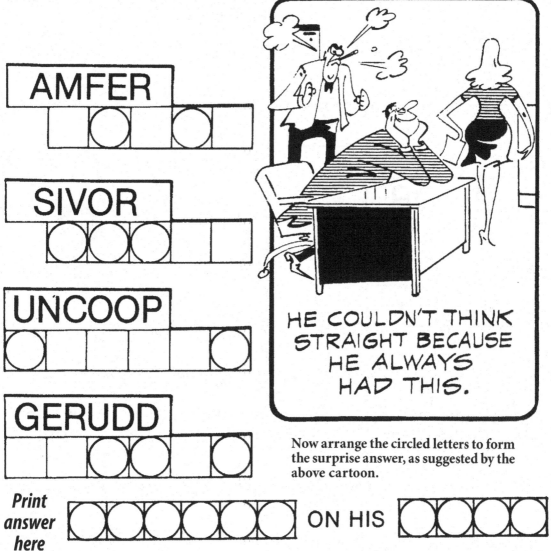

HE COULDN'T THINK STRAIGHT BECAUSE HE ALWAYS HAD THIS.

Now arrange the circled letters to form the surprise answer, as suggested by the above cartoon.

Print answer here ◯◯◯◯◯◯ ON HIS ◯◯◯◯

PUZZLE 86

JUMBLE®

Unscramble these four Jumbles, one letter to each square, to form four ordinary words.

GILTH

BEPOR

DUNCIE

MOABEA

SOME PEOPLE WHO DON'T PAY TAXES IN DUE TIME—

Now arrange the circled letters to form the surprise answer, as suggested by the above cartoon.

Print answer here

PUZZLE 87

JUMBLE®

Unscramble these four Jumbles, one letter to each square, to form four ordinary words.

ACEEP

YATHS

HISRAP

CUSPER

WHAT YOU MIGHT FIND IN AN AUTO-MOBILE GRAVEYARD.

Now arrange the circled letters to form the surprise answer, as suggested by the above cartoon.

Print answer here ◯◯◯◯◯ OF "◯◯◯◯◯"

PUZZLE 88

JUMBLE®

Unscramble these four Jumbles, one letter to each square, to form four ordinary words.

LOVEN

REGUP

YALMIN

TECJOB

WHAT THE GUARD CALLED THE KEY TO THE JAIL, AS HE THREW IT AWAY.

Now arrange the circled letters to form the surprise answer, as suggested by the above cartoon.

Print answer here THE

PUZZLE 89

JUMBLE®

Unscramble these four Jumbles, one letter to each square, to form four ordinary words.

HOTOT

GUBOS

TICUND

CYRIKT

THEY DRANK TO EACH OTHER'S HEALTH SO OFTEN THAT THIS HAPPENED.

Now arrange the circled letters to form the surprise answer, as suggested by the above cartoon.

Print answer here

PUZZLE 90

JUMBLE®

Unscramble these four Jumbles, one letter to each square, to form four ordinary words.

NORIM

FRAWE

ROSABB

SQUOME

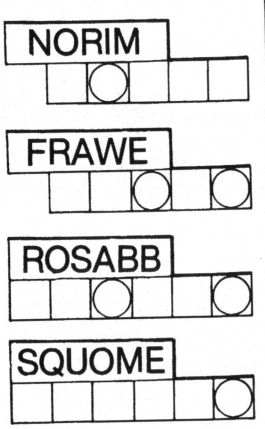

WHAT BRIEFS ARE USUALLY "WOVEN" FROM.

Now arrange the circled letters to form the surprise answer, as suggested by the above cartoon.

Print answer here " "

PUZZLE
91

JUMBLE®

Unscramble these four Jumbles, one letter to each square, to form four ordinary words.

LEVVA

AMMAD

CHEWEN

DRIFOL

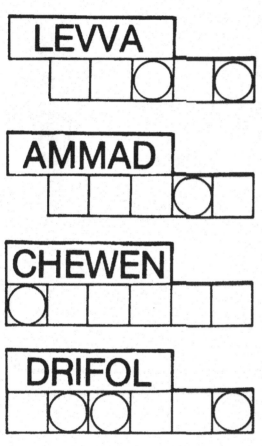

We're all in the same boat these days
PAY LOANS HERE

EVERYBODY WAS IN DEBT BUT IT'S PERMITTED.

Now arrange the circled letters to form the surprise answer, as suggested by the above cartoon.

Print answer here "___-____"

PUZZLE 92

JUMBLE®

Unscramble these four Jumbles, one letter to each square, to form four ordinary words.

STURY

THANC

FORTYS

SHIVAL

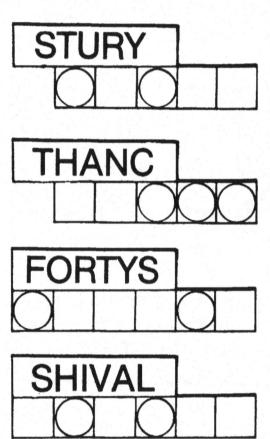

What! No food for such a long trip?
I'm hungry!

WHAT IT TURNED OUT TO BE WHEN THEY FORGOT TO HOOK ON THE DINING CAR.

Now arrange the circled letters to form the surprise answer, as suggested by the above cartoon.

Print answer here A "   "

PUZZLE
93

JUMBLE®

Unscramble these four Jumbles, one letter to each square, to form four ordinary words.

DRYBE

LORGY

DELNAH

FIGNAC

7/28
SOUNDS LIKE A FISHERMAN'S DANCE.

Now arrange the circled letters to form the surprise answer, as suggested by the above cartoon.

Print answer here

PUZZLE 94

JUMBLE®

Unscramble these four Jumbles, one letter to each square, to form four ordinary words.

SOEBE

DYRYL

CROLIF

NIDIOE

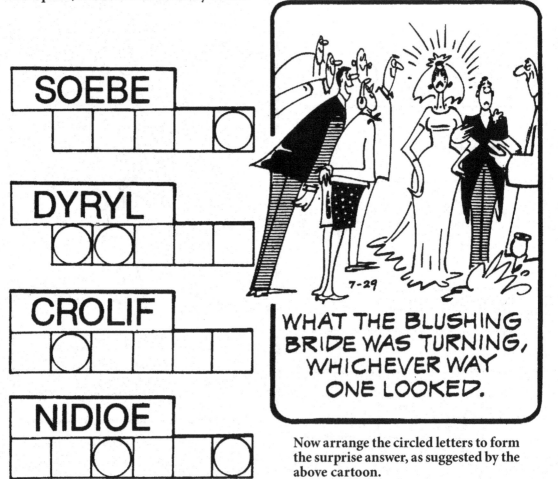

WHAT THE BLUSHING BRIDE WAS TURNING, WHICHEVER WAY ONE LOOKED.

Now arrange the circled letters to form the surprise answer, as suggested by the above cartoon.

Print answer here

PUZZLE 95

JUMBLE®

Unscramble these four Jumbles, one letter to each square, to form four ordinary words.

CAMIG

GUVEA

TRAFYC

SAUNAE

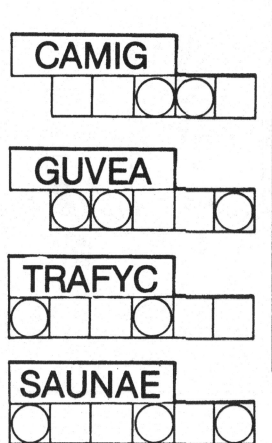

How's he gonna get out of THIS one?

WHAT A PERSON WHO LOSES HIS HEAD WOULD HAVE DIFFICULTY DOING.

Now arrange the circled letters to form the surprise answer, as suggested by the above cartoon.

Print answer here

PUZZLE 96

JUMBLE®

Unscramble these four Jumbles, one letter to each square, to form four ordinary words.

The traffic was murder today
HOW THE EXECU- TIONER WOULD HAVE PREFERRED GETTING TO WORK.

RYMEC

NYPOH

NIRBON

CIPTED

Now arrange the circled letters to form the surprise answer, as suggested by the above cartoon.

Print answer here

PUZZLE 97

JUMBLE®

Unscramble these four Jumbles, one letter to each square, to form four ordinary words.

WATHE

RADIC

ROMMEY

FLAUWL

Goody—blubber!
8-9
WHAT THOSE ESKIMOS LOVED TO DO AT DINNERTIME.

Now arrange the circled letters to form the surprise answer, as suggested by the above cartoon.

Print answer here ◯◯◯◯ THE ◯◯◯

PUZZLE 98

JUMBLE®

Unscramble these four Jumbles, one letter to each square, to form four ordinary words.

HACOP

GOMOR

GROINI

RUMAID

But he pulls in plenty
WHAT SOME COMEDIANS MAKE.

Now arrange the circled letters to form the surprise answer, as suggested by the above cartoon.

Print answer here ☐☐☐☐☐ OUT OF ☐☐☐☐

PUZZLE 99

JUMBLE®

Unscramble these four Jumbles, one letter to each square, to form four ordinary words.

HYBUS

KONET

PEKAUM

HINGAC

WHAT IT WAS FOR HIM WHEN THEY REPOSSESSED THE TV.

Now arrange the circled letters to form the surprise answer, as suggested by the above cartoon.

Print answer here A "   "

PUZZLE 100

JUMBLE®

Unscramble these four Jumbles, one letter to each square, to form four ordinary words.

ENSOO

CROAH

DROWPE

YEARTT

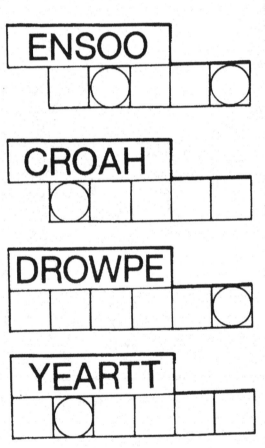

Oh, oh. . . we blew it!
DOWN WITH
A MISTAKE FOUND IN TERRORISM.

Now arrange the circled letters to form the surprise answer, as suggested by the above cartoon.

Print answer here " "

PUZZLE 101

JUMBLE®

Unscramble these four Jumbles, one letter to each square, to form four ordinary words.

TRYAR

ALTEM

NUCHAH

FROMIN

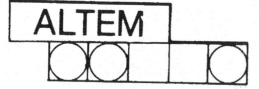

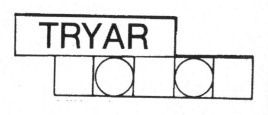

SCREECH!
CLANG
WHAT A REAL FIRM MAKES THAT MAY GO OFF IN THE HEAT.

Now arrange the circled letters to form the surprise answer, as suggested by the above cartoon.

Print answer here A " ◯◯◯◯ ◯◯◯◯◯ "

PUZZLE 102

JUMBLE®

Unscramble these four Jumbles, one letter to each square, to form four ordinary words.

BUJOM

ACOOC

NORMAT

DARZIL

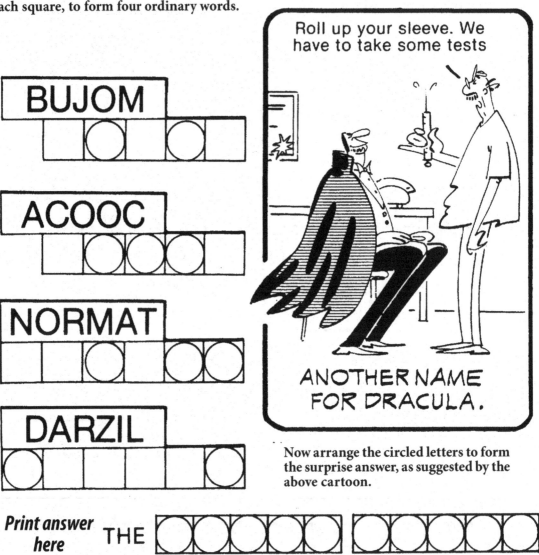

Roll up your sleeve. We have to take some tests
ANOTHER NAME FOR DRACULA.

Now arrange the circled letters to form the surprise answer, as suggested by the above cartoon.

Print answer here THE

PUZZLE 103

JUMBLE®

Unscramble these four Jumbles, one letter to each square, to form four ordinary words.

NOPIA

STULY

COAMIS

GLERCY

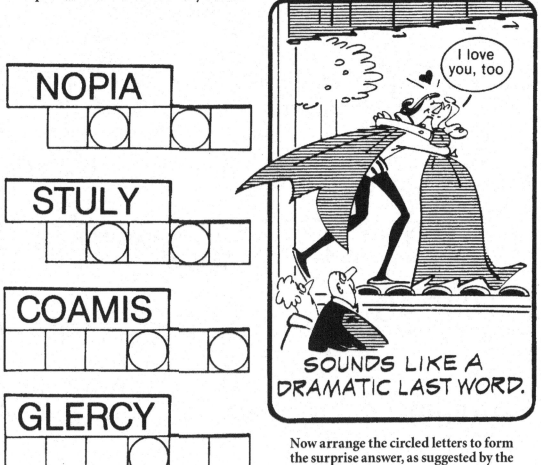

I love you, too
SOUNDS LIKE A DRAMATIC LAST WORD.

Now arrange the circled letters to form the surprise answer, as suggested by the above cartoon.

Print answer here " "

PUZZLE 104

JUMBLE®

Unscramble these four Jumbles, one letter to each square, to form four ordinary words.

BYBOH

OSSUE

HUMBAS

FANNIT

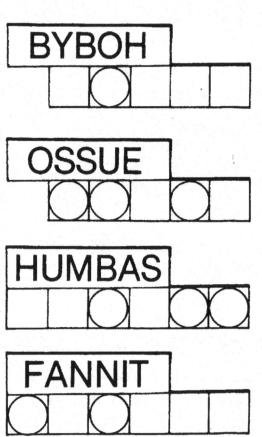

An intellectual
That ain't all!

HE HAS SUCCEEDED IN BUSINESS BY BEING A MAN OF GREAT CULTIVATION—

Now arrange the circled letters to form the surprise answer, as suggested by the above cartoon.

Print answer here

PUZZLE 105

JUMBLE®

Unscramble these four Jumbles, one letter to each square, to form four ordinary words.

AKELY

BELZA

HUBBYC

COIPLE

USING THIS, A GOLFER SHOULD KEEP THE FIRST PART ON THE SECOND.

Now arrange the circled letters to form the surprise answer, as suggested by the above cartoon.

Print answer here " ___ - ____ "

PUZZLE 106

JUMBLE®

Unscramble these four Jumbles, one letter to each square, to form four ordinary words.

SYLOU

ASTEE

ILCAME

REHFIE

WHAT THE POTTER'S ART CONSISTS OF.

Now arrange the circled letters to form the surprise answer, as suggested by the above cartoon.

Print answer here " ◯◯◯◯◯ " OF ◯◯◯◯

PUZZLE 107

JUMBLE®

Unscramble these four Jumbles, one letter to each square, to form four ordinary words.

ALZEH

CLAWR

STOFFE

HOMARI

I don't want any guessing
ARITHMETIC QUIZ TODAY
WHEN YOU GIVE THE ANSWERS IN "ROUND" NUMBERS, YOU'RE APT TO COME UP WITH THIS.

Now arrange the circled letters to form the surprise answer, as suggested by the above cartoon.

Print answer here

PUZZLE 108

JUMBLE®

Unscramble these four Jumbles, one letter to each square, to form four ordinary words.

TRIHM

KARNC

SHERTH

RUFIAN

But, m'sieur, are you a Frenchman?
LES ELECTIONS

HIS "POSITION" IN *FRANCE* GIVES HIM THE RIGHT TO VOTE.

Now arrange the circled letters to form the surprise answer, as suggested by the above cartoon.

Print answer here " ☐☐☐☐☐ - ☐☐☐ - ☐ "

PUZZLE 109

JUMBLE®

Unscramble these four Jumbles, one letter to each square, to form four ordinary words.

EVAUM

TILIM

WEEYAL

ALESEW

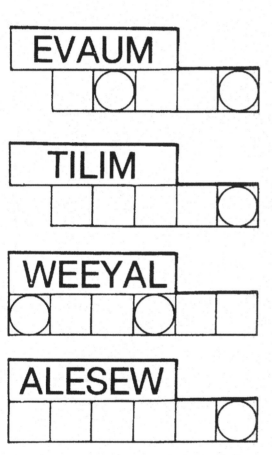

EVERYTHING IS "SOAKED" IN THE BILLFOLD.

Now arrange the circled letters to form the surprise answer, as suggested by the above cartoon.

Print answer here "[ ]-[ ][ ][ ]-[ ][ ]"

PUZZLE
110

JUMBLE®

Unscramble these four Jumbles, one letter to each square, to form four ordinary words.

PLITO

LOGAT

VIEWLS

BRUHEC

Oh, she doesn't know me anymore

AN INSULT THAT SOMETIMES SEEMS RATHER SLIGHT.

Now arrange the circled letters to form the surprise answer, as suggested by the above cartoon.

Print answer here “ ”

PUZZLE 111

JUMBLE®

Unscramble these four Jumbles, one letter to each square, to form four ordinary words.

UNREP

DULGI

BENRAY

CIANAM

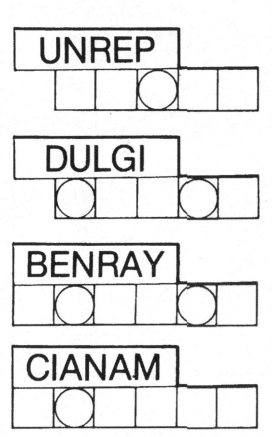

WHAT YOU MIGHT GET WHEN YOU OVERLY INDULGE.

Now arrange the circled letters to form the surprise answer, as suggested by the above cartoon.

Print answer here

PUZZLE 112

JUMBLE®

Unscramble these four Jumbles, one letter to each square, to form four ordinary words.

ANCOP

YAWNT

CLOIPY

RUBBGY

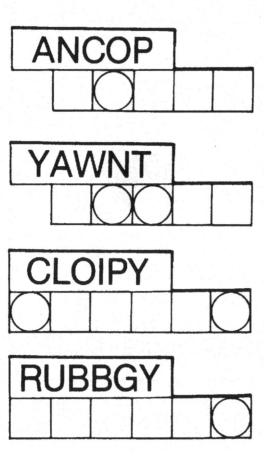

MANY PEOPLE BUY ON TIME, BUT FEW DO THIS.

Now arrange the circled letters to form the surprise answer, as suggested by the above cartoon.

Print answer here ( ) ( ) ( ) THAT ( ) ( ) ( )

PUZZLE 113

JUMBLE®

Unscramble these four Jumbles, one letter to each square, to form four ordinary words.

VAHEY

YERFO

ALOONG

NATQUI

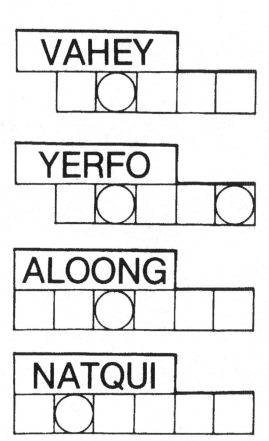

THIS SURE MADE HER FACE RED!

Now arrange the circled letters to form the surprise answer, as suggested by the above cartoon.

Print answer here

PUZZLE 114

JUMBLE®

Unscramble these four Jumbles, one letter to each square, to form four ordinary words.

TUPER

URSOE

SAUCCU

JELIAD

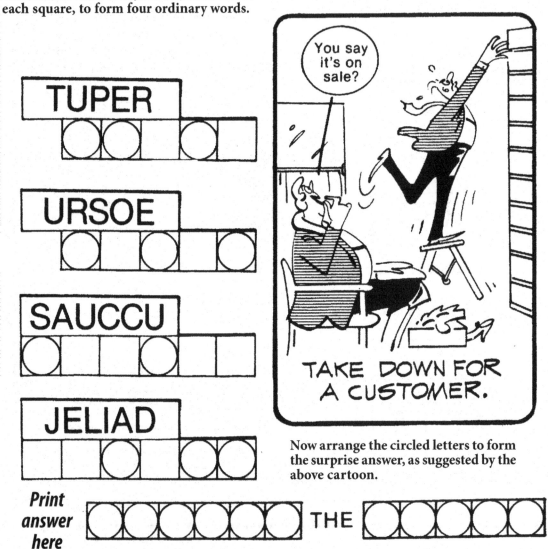

You say it's on sale?

TAKE DOWN FOR A CUSTOMER.

Now arrange the circled letters to form the surprise answer, as suggested by the above cartoon.

Print answer here ______ THE _____

PUZZLE
115

JUMBLE®

Unscramble these four Jumbles, one letter to each square, to form four ordinary words.

FECOR

EUNEQ

SOUXED

GOPINE

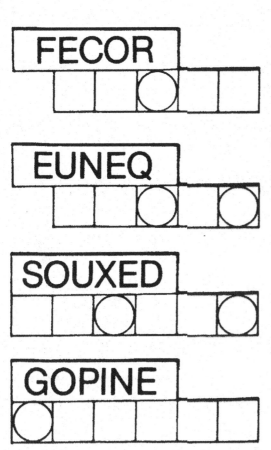

I AM THE FIRST ONE IN THE GRAMMAR CLASS
I DO WE DO
YOU DO THEY DO
HE, SHE, IT DOES
A

Now arrange the circled letters to form the surprise answer, as suggested by the above cartoon.

Print answer here " "

PUZZLE 116

JUMBLE®

Unscramble these four Jumbles, one letter to each square, to form four ordinary words.

NALTS

SOGOE

PITTYS

REWESK

She looks nervous

WHAT THE ANXIETY-RIDDEN SOPRANO WAS EVIDENTLY SUFFERING FROM.

Now arrange the circled letters to form the surprise answer, as suggested by the above cartoon.

Print answer here “____-______”

PUZZLE 117

JUMBLE®

Unscramble these four Jumbles, one letter to each square, to form four ordinary words.

NAYRE

OONNI

DOITUS

HYROTE

REWARD
TO
FINDER
9-19
WHAT HAPPENED TO THE FARMER'S CATTLE?

Now arrange the circled letters to form the surprise answer, as suggested by the above cartoon.

Print answer here

PUZZLE 118

JUMBLE®

Unscramble these four Jumbles, one letter to each square, to form four ordinary words.

TALEV

GAGBY

YOMARR

VOCENX

HOW THEY ACTED AT THE UNDERTAKERS' ANNUAL SHINDIG.

Now arrange the circled letters to form the surprise answer, as suggested by the above cartoon.

Print answer here

PUZZLE 119

JUMBLE®

Unscramble these four Jumbles, one letter to each square, to form four ordinary words.

HOACC

PREKO

TULYSS

YEEHRB

It's plagiarism!
It's not!
WHAT YOU MIGHT HAVE WHEN TWO AUTHORS SUE EACH OTHER.

Now arrange the circled letters to form the surprise answer, as suggested by the above cartoon.

Print answer here A

PUZZLE 120

JUMBLE®

Unscramble these four Jumbles, one letter to each square, to form four ordinary words.

DAGLE

PRYAT

CAGNEY

LIMBEN

WHAT A DENTIST MIGHT DO ABOUT THOSE MISSING TEETH.

Now arrange the circled letters to form the surprise answer, as suggested by the above cartoon.

Print answer here “ ” THE

PUZZLE
121

JUMBLE®

Unscramble these four Jumbles, one letter to each square, to form four ordinary words.

INSAB

KYDUS

NARXLY

PREDON

WHAT THE GARDENER SAID WHEN THE FLOWERS WOULDN'T GROW.

Now arrange the circled letters to form the surprise answer, as suggested by the above cartoon.

Print answer here " - "

PUZZLE 122

JUMBLE®

Unscramble these four Jumbles, one letter to each square, to form four ordinary words.

RILLT

NUBOD

VOGNER

BERBOR

CLANG!
CLANG!
WHAT THE LOCKSMITH MADE WHEN HIS SHOP CAUGHT FIRE.

Now arrange the circled letters to form the surprise answer, as suggested by the above cartoon.

Print answer here A ◯◯◯◯ FOR THE ◯◯◯◯

PUZZLE 123

JUMBLE®

Unscramble these four Jumbles, one letter to each square, to form four ordinary words.

NYSAP

FRACT

BUHLEM

BREMME

WHAT DID THEY ENGRAVE ON THE ROBOT'S TOMBSTONE?

Now arrange the circled letters to form the surprise answer, as suggested by the above cartoon.

Print answer here ☐☐☐☐ IN ☐☐☐☐☐

PUZZLE 124

JUMBLE®

Unscramble these four Jumbles, one letter to each square, to form four ordinary words.

DEYNE

YURUS

ONCOMM

SHRAID

WHAT SHE TOLD HER COWBOY FRIEND NOT TO DO.

Now arrange the circled letters to form the surprise answer, as suggested by the above cartoon.

Print answer here

PUZZLE 125

JUMBLE®

Unscramble these four Jumbles, one letter to each square, to form four ordinary words.

SASIB

PALLE

MERMAH

BOALIN

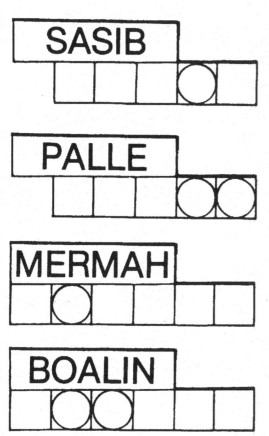

My client demands full restitution for what he wrote
OBLIGATED ACCORDING TO LAW WHEN YOU "CONCOCT" A LIBEL.

Now arrange the circled letters to form the surprise answer, as suggested by the above cartoon.

Print answer here " "

PUZZLE 126

JUMBLE®

Unscramble these four Jumbles, one letter to each square, to form four ordinary words.

GOWAN

NIYKK

LOICAS

BLOUED

WHAT HAPPENED TO THE MAN WHO INVENTED VANISHING CREAM?

Now arrange the circled letters to form the surprise answer, as suggested by the above cartoon.

Print answer here

PUZZLE 127

JUMBLE®

Unscramble these four Jumbles, one letter to each square, to form four ordinary words.

ENFLO

AKNEW

WOAMED

ROHRRO

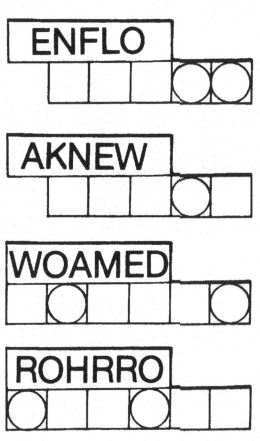

Where's that waiter? One minute he's here and the next he's gone!
PRESENT AT PRESENT BUT NOT PRESENT.

Now arrange the circled letters to form the surprise answer, as suggested by the above cartoon.

Print answer here "○○○-○○○○"

PUZZLE 128

JUMBLE®

Unscramble these four Jumbles, one letter to each square, to form four ordinary words.

KRIHE

LODOF

PANMEC

LEEXUD

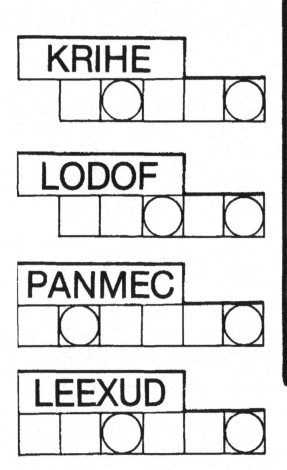

WHAT SHE TOLD HER HUSBAND HE HAD BETTER DO WHILE ON THAT FISHING TRIP.

Now arrange the circled letters to form the surprise answer, as suggested by the above cartoon.

Print answer here ◯◯◯◯ A ◯◯◯◯

PUZZLE 129

JUMBLE®

Unscramble these four Jumbles, one letter to each square, to form four ordinary words.

LAWZT

PUPER

ENNKLE

YAWNAY

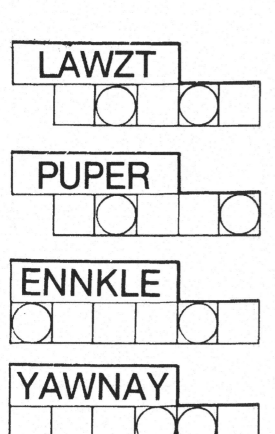

WHEN HE SAW THE COPS, THE ROBBER TOOK OFF AND LEFT HIS ACCOMPLICE TO DO THIS.

Now arrange the circled letters to form the surprise answer, as suggested by the above cartoon.

Print answer here ☐☐☐☐ THE "☐☐☐☐☐"

PUZZLE 130

JUMBLE®

Unscramble these four Jumbles, one letter to each square, to form four ordinary words.

PYKER

GWEED

RADACE

GREEME

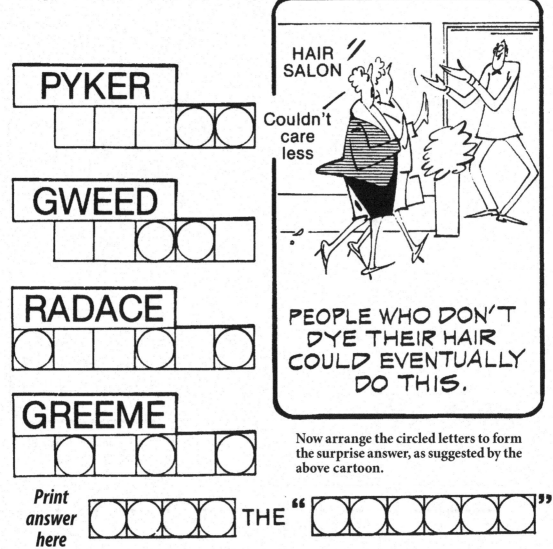

HAIR SALON
Couldn't care less
PEOPLE WHO DON'T DYE THEIR HAIR COULD EVENTUALLY DO THIS.

Now arrange the circled letters to form the surprise answer, as suggested by the above cartoon.

Print answer here THE " "

PUZZLE 131

JUMBLE®

Unscramble these four Jumbles, one letter to each square, to form four ordinary words.

PALPY

LURBY

MYFAIL

GLUNJE

THE KANGAROO VISITED A SHRINK BECAUSE HE HAD BEEN FEELING THIS LATELY.

Now arrange the circled letters to form the surprise answer, as suggested by the above cartoon.

Print answer here

PUZZLE 132

JUMBLE®

Unscramble these four Jumbles, one letter to each square, to form four ordinary words.

KULFE

COAME

AFAIRS

NOGARD

Hi, pal
FRANKENSTEIN WAS LONELY UNTIL HE DISCOVERED HOW TO DO THIS.

Now arrange the circled letters to form the surprise answer, as suggested by the above cartoon.

Print answer here

PUZZLE 133

JUMBLE®

Unscramble these four Jumbles, one letter to each square, to form four ordinary words.

REBBI

KLANF

YOMFID

CINTAG

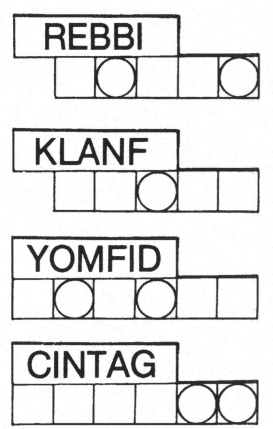

Saves me so much work

WHEN THEY INVENTED DRIP-DRY CLOTHES, THIS JUST ABOUT CAME TO AN END.

Now arrange the circled letters to form the surprise answer, as suggested by the above cartoon.

Print answer here THE ○○○○ ○○○

PUZZLE

134

JUMBLE®

Unscramble these four Jumbles, one letter to each square, to form four ordinary words.

WOPER

TABOL

CLAFIA

VELCOR

WHAT HAPPENED WHEN HE PUT DYNAMITE INTO THE REFRIGERATOR?

Now arrange the circled letters to form the surprise answer, as suggested by the above cartoon.

Print answer here HE ◯◯◯◯ HIS ◯◯◯◯

PUZZLE 135

JUMBLE®

Unscramble these four Jumbles, one letter to each square, to form four ordinary words.

TYKIT

ENNIL

PERMAC

ONSOAL

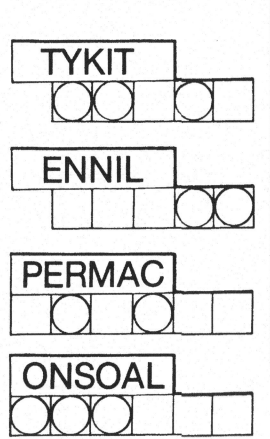

I come to bury Caesar. . .
WHAT THE ANCIENT ROMANS COULD DO EASILY THAT MOST MODERNS HAVE DIFFICULTY DOING.

Now arrange the circled letters to form the surprise answer, as suggested by the above cartoon.

Print answer here

PUZZLE 136

JUMBLE®

Unscramble these four Jumbles, one letter to each square, to form four ordinary words.

ENVIL

LIDUF

INGINN

FEEDAM

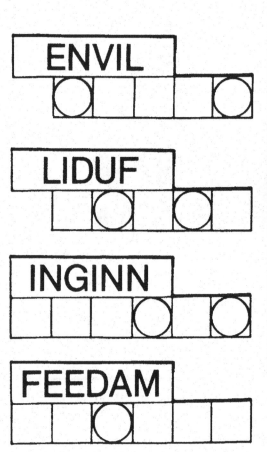

THE DENTIST GREW FAT BECAUSE ALMOST EVERYTHING HE TOUCHED WAS THIS.

Now arrange the circled letters to form the surprise answer, as suggested by the above cartoon.

Print answer here

PUZZLE 137

JUMBLE®

Unscramble these four Jumbles, one letter to each square, to form four ordinary words.

OPTIA

ROUCS

CARCIT

CATIMP

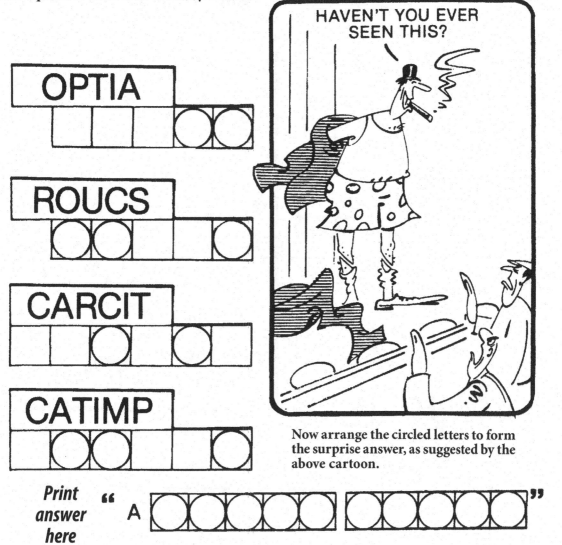

HAVEN'T YOU EVER SEEN THIS?

Now arrange the circled letters to form the surprise answer, as suggested by the above cartoon.

Print answer here "A ______ ______"

PUZZLE 138

JUMBLE®

Unscramble these four Jumbles, one letter to each square, to form four ordinary words.

CENUD

DAUGY

TRIVEN

DOLIBY

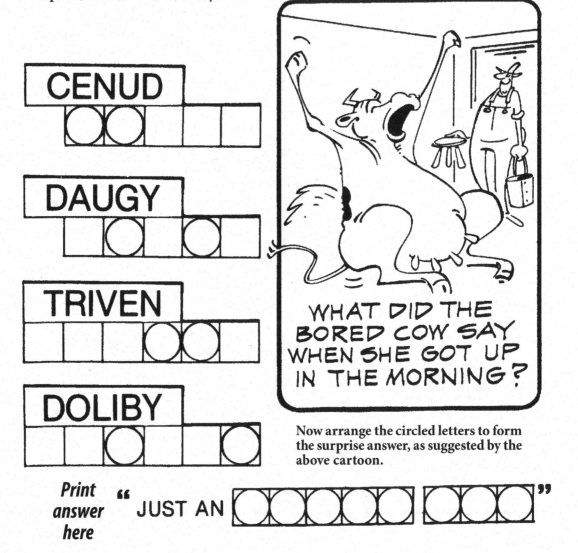

WHAT DID THE BORED COW SAY WHEN SHE GOT UP IN THE MORNING?

Now arrange the circled letters to form the surprise answer, as suggested by the above cartoon.

Print answer here "JUST AN"

PUZZLE 139

JUMBLE®

Unscramble these four Jumbles, one letter to each square, to form four ordinary words.

THICY

KAFLE

FELDIE

RUSLAW

AFTER ANOTHER WOMAN HAD "TURNED" HIS HEAD, HE OBVIOUSLY COULDN'T DO THIS ANYMORE.

Now arrange the circled letters to form the surprise answer, as suggested by the above cartoon.

Print answer here ◯◯◯◯ HIS ◯◯◯◯

PUZZLE 140

JUMBLE®

Unscramble these four Jumbles, one letter to each square, to form four ordinary words.

MAGLE

TINGY

RAYNPT

MESHEC

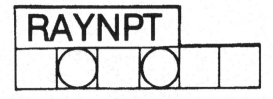

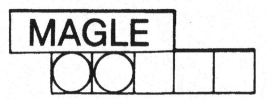

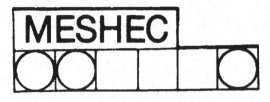

HOW DOES A BABY CHICK FIT INTO ITS SHELL?

Now arrange the circled letters to form the surprise answer, as suggested by the above cartoon.

Print answer here " "

PUZZLE 141

JUMBLE®

Unscramble these four Jumbles, one letter to each square, to form four ordinary words.

ENYAH

NURSP

YULIBS

DEMOAP

WHAT DO YOU GET WHEN YOU CROSS A CACTUS WITH A PORCUPINE?

Now arrange the circled letters to form the surprise answer, as suggested by the above cartoon.

Print answer here

PUZZLE 142

JUMBLE

Unscramble these four Jumbles, one letter to each square, to form four ordinary words.

VIALE

ILVIC

THEIRE

AMBALS

HERE REPOSES
NEVER TOLD THE TRUTH IN HIS LIFE
WHAT DO LIARS DO AFTER THEY DIE?

Now arrange the circled letters to form the surprise answer, as suggested by the above cartoon.

Print answer here

PUZZLE 143

JUMBLE®

Unscramble these four Jumbles, one letter to each square, to form four ordinary words.

NAGET

BLAYK

DANNIL

SEBIED

WHAT BRINGS FLOWERS?

Now arrange the circled letters to form the surprise answer, as suggested by the above cartoon.

Print answer here THE " "

PUZZLE 144

JUMBLE®

Unscramble these four Jumbles, one letter to each square, to form four ordinary words.

YILSK

ENPOY

ENCAME

DEGUMS

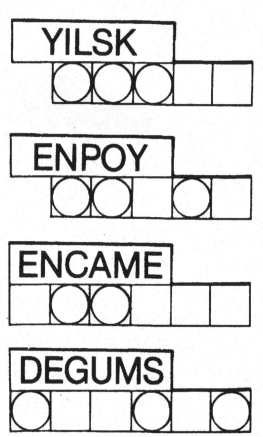

WHAT SHOULD A SWORD SWALLOWER EAT WHEN HE'S ON A DIET?

Now arrange the circled letters to form the surprise answer, as suggested by the above cartoon.

Print answer here &

PUZZLE 145

JUMBLE®

Unscramble these four Jumbles, one letter to each square, to form four ordinary words.

WOSON

RIGMY

TREENI

ANGAME

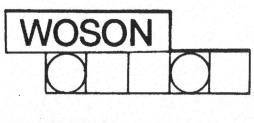

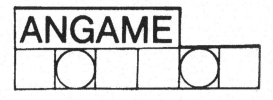

Some job getting her off our hands!
COULD BE INSTRUMENTAL IN A MARRIAGE.

Now arrange the circled letters to form the surprise answer, as suggested by the above cartoon.

Print answer here THE

PUZZLE 146

JUMBLE®

Unscramble these four Jumbles, one letter to each square, to form four ordinary words.

KESTO

TULDA

CUBLEK

CISEXE

WHAT HAPPENED TO THE MAN WHO SUED THE PORTER?

Now arrange the circled letters to form the surprise answer, as suggested by the above cartoon.

Print answer here HE ◯◯◯◯ HIS ◯◯◯◯

PUZZLE 147

JUMBLE®

Unscramble these four Jumbles, one letter to each square, to form four ordinary words.

GUZAE

KWISH

UNGOAT

THAGUT

WHAT DO YOU CALL IT WHEN PIGS DO THEIR LAUNDRY?

Now arrange the circled letters to form the surprise answer, as suggested by the above cartoon.

Print answer here

PUZZLE 148

JUMBLE®

Unscramble these four Jumbles, one letter to each square, to form four ordinary words.

RUSUP

FONTE

PECTOK

ENLOOD

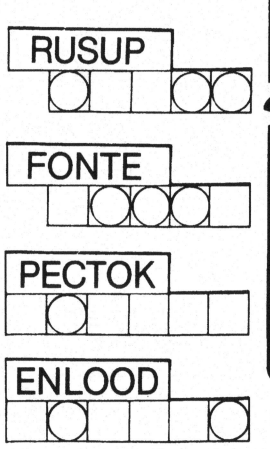

$
IF YOU WANT TO BUY A GOOD WIG, YOU SURE HAVE THIS.

Now arrange the circled letters to form the surprise answer, as suggested by the above cartoon.

Print answer here IT

PUZZLE 149

JUMBLE®

Unscramble these four Jumbles, one letter to each square, to form four ordinary words.

KLEAN

TYMPE

VEEBAH

NEAFED

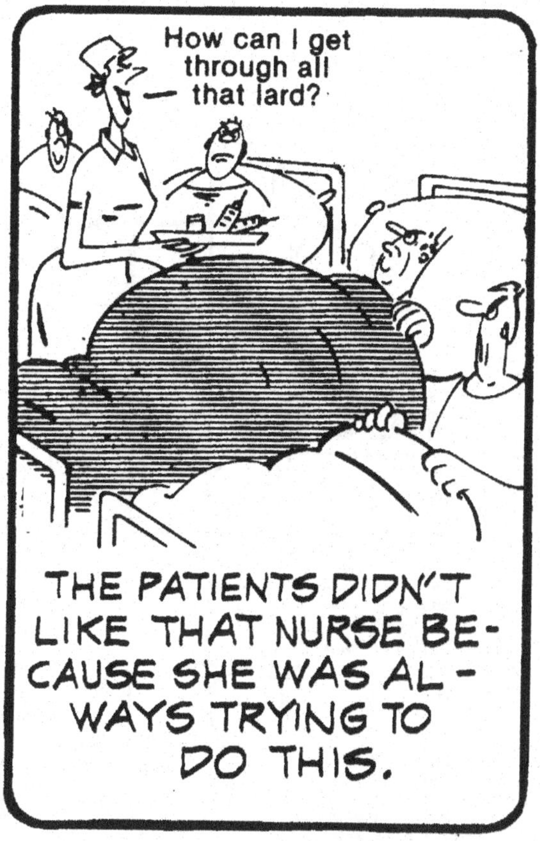
How can I get through all that lard?
THE PATIENTS DIDN'T LIKE THAT NURSE BE-CAUSE SHE WAS AL-WAYS TRYING TO DO THIS.

Now arrange the circled letters to form the surprise answer, as suggested by the above cartoon.

Print answer here

PUZZLE
150

JUMBLE®

Unscramble these four Jumbles, one letter to each square, to form four ordinary words.

TUBOA

NIDEK

DOBOLY

HINEAL

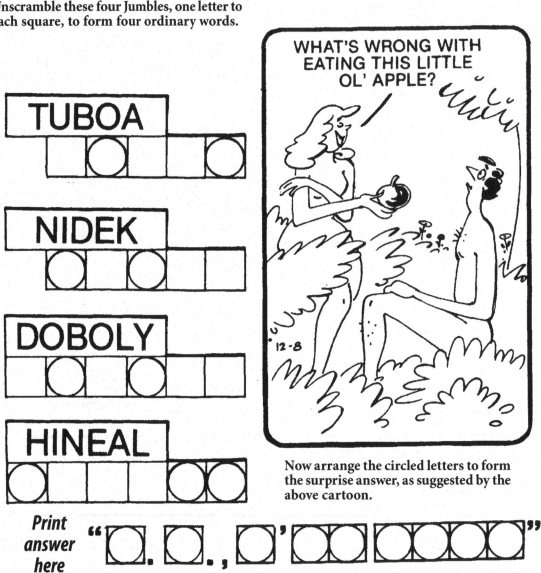

WHAT'S WRONG WITH EATING THIS LITTLE OL' APPLE?
12-8

Now arrange the circled letters to form the surprise answer, as suggested by the above cartoon.

Print answer here “ _ . _ . , _ ' _ _   _ _ _ _ _ ”

PUZZLE 151

JUMBLE®

Unscramble these four Jumbles, one letter to each square, to form four ordinary words.

LUTEX

UNORM

YULTIG

CAPELA

WHAT TEQUILA IS.

Now arrange the circled letters to form the surprise answer, as suggested by the above cartoon.

Print answer here THE "◯◯◯◯" OF ◯◯◯◯◯◯

PUZZLE 152

JUMBLE®

Unscramble these four Jumbles, one letter to each square, to form four ordinary words.

ATAGE

NOPER

CRYLEE

NEPAHP

CALENDAR
WHY NEXT YEAR IS A GOOD YEAR FOR KANGAROOS.

Now arrange the circled letters to form the surprise answer, as suggested by the above cartoon.

Print answer here IT'S " "

PUZZLE 153

JUMBLE®

Unscramble these four Jumbles, one letter to each square, to form four ordinary words.

DEWPI

TALAN

NEPTLY

ERRTAY

WHAT THE BIG GAME WAS WHEN THEY PUT THEIR STAR MUMMY IN AS PINCH HITTER.

Now arrange the circled letters to form the surprise answer, as suggested by the above cartoon.

Print answer here

PUZZLE 154

JUMBLE®

Unscramble these four Jumbles, one letter to each square, to form four ordinary words.

NIORB

POUMI

REYGES

GENJAL

Number one—that's me!
THIS WAS THE GRAND WAY IN WHICH SHE PROCLAIMED THAT SHE WAS A TOP MODEL.

Now arrange the circled letters to form the surprise answer, as suggested by the above cartoon.

Print answer here " ' - "

PUZZLE 155

JUMBLE®

Unscramble these four Jumbles, one letter to each square, to form four ordinary words.

RATAO

ULIGE

TUPSID

LAHMYN

Oh, what a night
WHAT KIND OF AN EXPERIENCE WAS IT WHEN HE LOOKED INTO THE MIRROR?

Now arrange the circled letters to form the surprise answer, as suggested by the above cartoon.

Print answer here A ○○○○○○○○○○ ONE

PUZZLE 156

JUMBLE®

Unscramble these four Jumbles, one letter to each square, to form four ordinary words.

DUNET

YIEPT

TRONIA

MEETOL

WHAT THE AMBASSADOR'S DOG CERTAINLY WAS NOT.

Now arrange the circled letters to form the surprise answer, as suggested by the above cartoon.

Print answer here A "_ _ _ _ _ - _ _ _ _"

PUZZLE 157

JUMBLE®

Unscramble these four Jumbles, one letter to each square, to form four ordinary words.

HARNC

LAIGE

DOULCY

ENGLIS

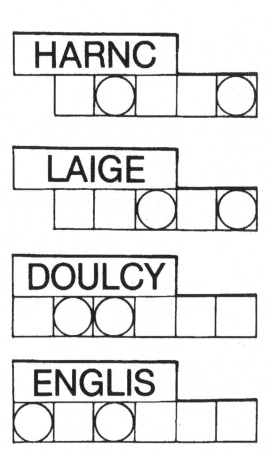

WHAT GOES UP THE STAIRS ON ITS HEAD?

Now arrange the circled letters to form the surprise answer, as suggested by the above cartoon.

Print answer here A ◯◯◯◯ IN A ◯◯◯◯

PUZZLE 158

JUMBLE®

Unscramble these four Jumbles, one letter to each square, to form four ordinary words.

MULBA

STOFI

PHEPOR

TOLBET

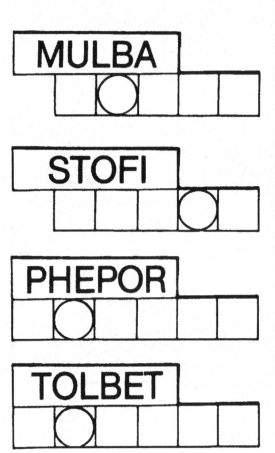

HOW COULD SHE SING SO HIGH WHEN SHE WAS THIS?

Now arrange the circled letters to form the surprise answer, as suggested by the above cartoon.

Print answer here " "

PUZZLE 159

JUMBLE®

Unscramble these four Jumbles, one letter to each square, to form four ordinary words.

EUQIR

NOAGY

YADDLE

GENNIE

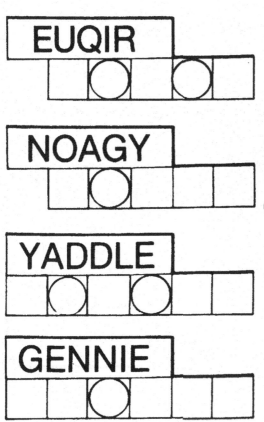

WHAT KIND OF AN EXPERIENCE IS IT TO TRAVEL BY FLYING CARPET?

Now arrange the circled letters to form the surprise answer, as suggested by the above cartoon.

Print answer here A ○○○○○○ ONE

PUZZLE 160

JUMBLE®

Unscramble these four Jumbles, one letter to each square, to form four ordinary words.

BUNGE

COVAL

REPIME

YEMMAH

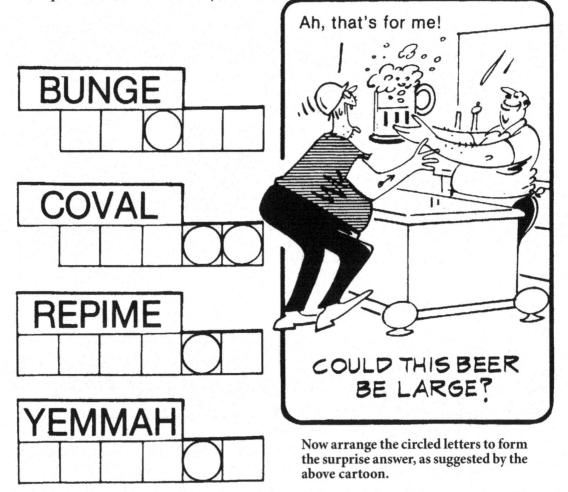

Ah, that's for me!
COULD THIS BEER BE LARGE?

Now arrange the circled letters to form the surprise answer, as suggested by the above cartoon.

Print answer here " ◯◯◯◯◯ "

JUMBLE®

MARATHON

Challenger Puzzles

PUZZLE 161

JUMBLE®

Unscramble these six Jumbles, one letter to each square, to form six ordinary words.

LONPEL

LOMBIE

BINNOR

ROTHAX

HELAGG

LEMOTE

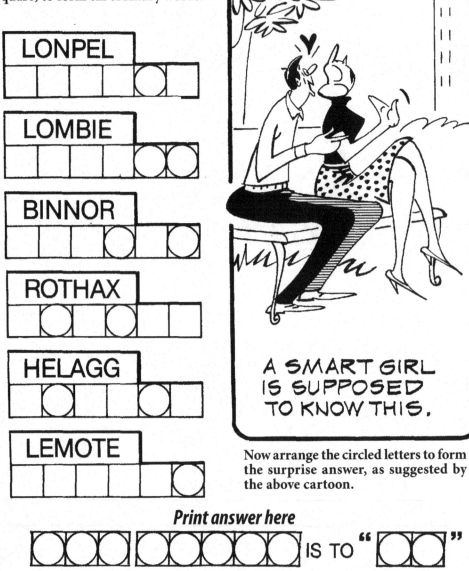

A SMART GIRL IS SUPPOSED TO KNOW THIS.

Now arrange the circled letters to form the surprise answer, as suggested by the above cartoon.

Print answer here

◯◯◯ ◯◯◯◯◯ IS TO "◯◯"

PUZZLE 162

JUMBLE®

Unscramble these six Jumbles, one letter to each square, to form six ordinary words.

BABFLY

VERHIT

YAMSIL

MANCEP

OKOCIE

TANIAT

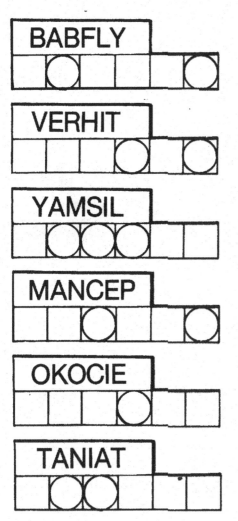

Must be in a hurry

HOW THEY ATE THAT FANCY BANANA AND ICE CREAM DISH.

Now arrange the circled letters to form the surprise answer, as suggested by the above cartoon.

Print answer here

PUZZLE 163

JUMBLE®

Unscramble these six Jumbles, one letter to each square, to form six ordinary words.

SWEFET

MYLODE

GLOBON

DOWHAS

YERRAP

WOUTTI

Don't repeat this, but. . .
WHAT A LADIES' LOUNGE MIGHT BE CALLED.

Now arrange the circled letters to form the surprise answer, as suggested by the above cartoon.

Print answer here

A "_ _ _ _ _ _-_ _ _" _ _ _ _ _

PUZZLE 164

JUMBLE®

Unscramble these six Jumbles, one letter to each square, to form six ordinary words.

SIMREY

FRILPE

ARUSSE

ENCHEW

TYRITH

ZANATS

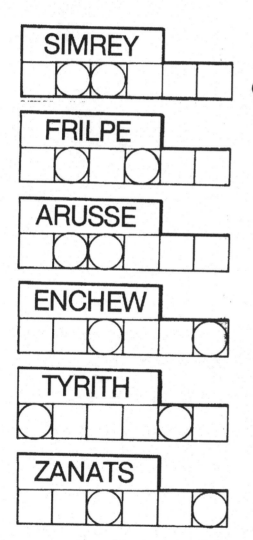

WHAT AN OLDSTER SOMETIMES PREFERS.

Now arrange the circled letters to form the surprise answer, as suggested by the above cartoon.

Print answer here

A ______ TO A ______

PUZZLE 165

JUMBLE®

Unscramble these six Jumbles, one letter to each square, to form six ordinary words.

NARBER

THORCC

SAFRAC

HESKLE

BOYDEM

TEABED

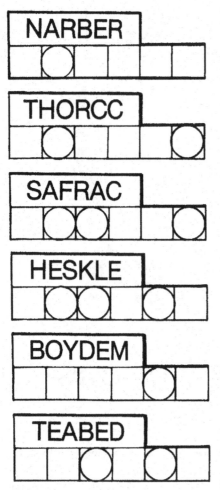

TANTIVY
TANTIVY
Whew!
HOW THE RABBIT MANAGED TO ESCAPE FROM THE HUNTERS.

Now arrange the circled letters to form the surprise answer, as suggested by the above cartoon.

Print answer here

BY A "____'_" _______

JUMBLE®

Unscramble these six Jumbles, one letter to each square, to form six ordinary words.

WELDIM

STUJYL

EEFELC

LORCAR

WUSBAY

MULASY

WHAT GRAFFITI ARE.

Now arrange the circled letters to form the surprise answer, as suggested by the above cartoon.

Print answer here

○○○○○○○ ON ○○○○○○

PUZZLE 167

JUMBLE®

Unscramble these six Jumbles, one letter to each square, to form six ordinary words.

ANDAGE

BAHCLE

UNOFSI

TRINWY

TEANIN

WANEDD

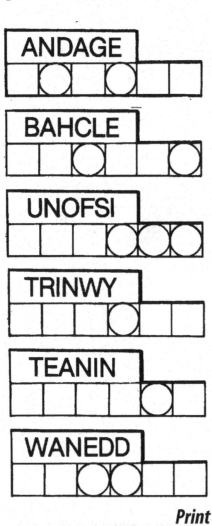

WHY THEY WERE BORED AT THE NUDIST CAMP.

Now arrange the circled letters to form the surprise answer, as suggested by the above cartoon.

Print answer here

ON THERE

PUZZLE 168

JUMBLE®

Unscramble these six Jumbles, one letter to each square, to form six ordinary words.

HURTOF

LESTED

YANBOT

RAJAUG

HIRAGS

DIONIE

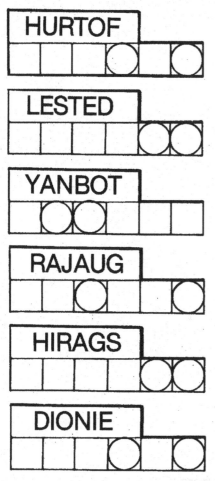

I'm bettin' on the guy in black
WHAT A SUCCESSFUL PRIZE FIGHTER USUALLY HAS TO CONSIDER.

Now arrange the circled letters to form the surprise answer, as suggested by the above cartoon.

Print answer here

THE "◯◯◯◯◯◯" OF ◯◯◯◯◯◯

PUZZLE 169

JUMBLE®

Unscramble these six Jumbles, one letter to each square, to form six ordinary words.

ROOHRR

GLYFAD

TULFIE

NEEXTT

NOCHOP

SORABB

Don't you think we should call a professional?

HOW SOME DO-IT-YOURSELF FREAKS ALWAYS SEEM TO FIX THINGS.

Now arrange the circled letters to form the surprise answer, as suggested by the above cartoon.

Print answer here

PUZZLE 170

JUMBLE®

Unscramble these six Jumbles, one letter to each square, to form six ordinary words.

DIPAUN

TOARRO

LUFOWE

SNIDUM

DREEME

GEJLUG

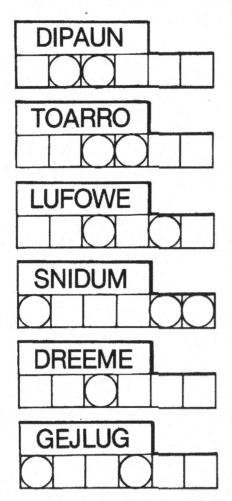

Got it!
CLICK!
WHAT A GOOD PHOTOGRAPHER OFTEN HAS TO KNOW HOW TO MAKE.

Now arrange the circled letters to form the surprise answer, as suggested by the above cartoon.

Print answer here

A “ ”

PUZZLE 171

JUMBLE®

Unscramble these six Jumbles, one letter to each square, to form six ordinary words.

MENECT

GROHPE

MARSID

LEZZUP

FLIECK

SHABIN

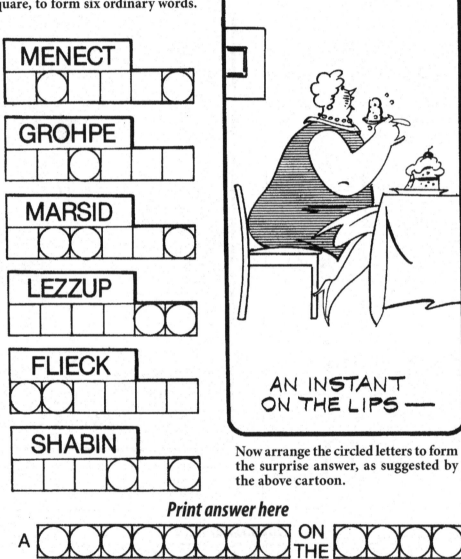

AN INSTANT
ON THE LIPS —

Now arrange the circled letters to form the surprise answer, as suggested by the above cartoon.

Print answer here

A ○○○○○○○○ ON THE ○○○○○

PUZZLE 172

JUMBLE®

Unscramble these six Jumbles, one letter to each square, to form six ordinary words.

RAHGEC

LOWLAF

BURGYB

COZADI

YARROS

KLANTE

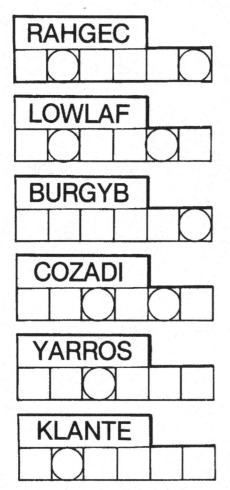

WHAT KIND OF A CHARACTER WAS THE GUY WHO WAS LYING UNDER A TREE WATCHING HIS WIFE MOW THE LAWN?

Now arrange the circled letters to form the surprise answer, as suggested by the above cartoon.

Print answer here

PUZZLE 173

JUMBLE®

Unscramble these six Jumbles, one letter to each square, to form six ordinary words.

SNORPI

TOUTLE

SLEAWE

IMVOTE

CROFIL

HYBBUC

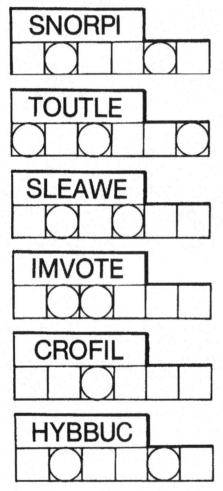

THAT SHOE SALESMAN HAS ONE WOMAN WHO'S HIS STEADY, AND MANY THIS.

Now arrange the circled letters to form the surprise answer, as suggested by the above cartoon.

Print answer here

PUZZLE 174

JUMBLE®

Unscramble these six Jumbles, one letter to each square, to form six ordinary words.

PALLAP

YENICT

DAMALY

PANPHE

MUPCIE

LAUTRI

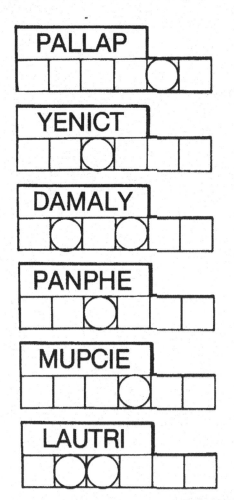

I'm self-made
Yeah—and with the aid of a rich uncle
WHAT THE CAPITAL OF THAT EGOTISTICAL MILLIONAIRE MOSTLY WAS.

Now arrange the circled letters to form the surprise answer, as suggested by the above cartoon.

Print answer here

PUZZLE 175

JUMBLE®

Unscramble these six Jumbles, one letter to each square, to form six ordinary words.

RUBECH

LABBED

MINUME

IMDOYF

BLUHME

LUPPIT

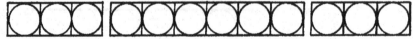

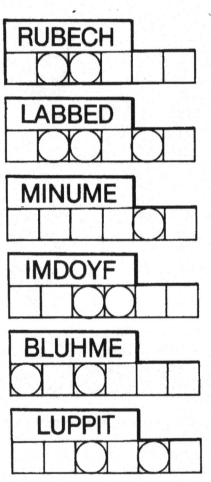

WHERE THE SCHOOL BUS DRIVER'S PROBLEMS WERE.

Now arrange the circled letters to form the surprise answer, as suggested by the above cartoon.

Print answer here

PUZZLE 176

JUMBLE®

Unscramble these six Jumbles, one letter to each square, to form six ordinary words.

BRYDOW

EMVOIT

BIDROF

MYPLOC

TIPSEC

SHRUPE

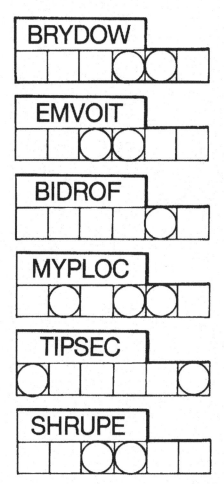

WHAT YOU MIGHT FIND AT A HAUNTED COLLEGE.

Now arrange the circled letters to form the surprise answer, as suggested by the above cartoon.

Print answer here

SOME ______ " ______ "

PUZZLE 177

JUMBLE®

Unscramble these six Jumbles, one letter to each square, to form six ordinary words.

MASHAT

CLUSIE

SHOMAN

DENCUF

NAIVED

ABLEED

WHAT A SUCCESSFUL BOOKSELLER HOPES TO DO.

Now arrange the circled letters to form the surprise answer, as suggested by the above cartoon.

Print answer here

PUZZLE 178

JUMBLE®

Unscramble these six Jumbles, one letter to each square, to form six ordinary words.

GEELUM

INJEYT

NOBIAL

DINKLY

AUGIAN

GRACIT

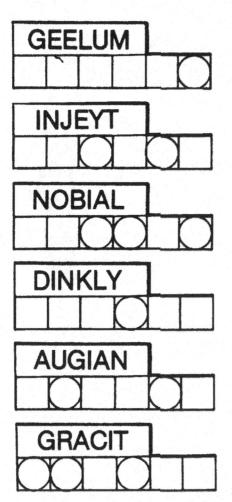

WHAT DID THE TREE SAY AFTER THE WOOD-PECKER PECKED AWAY AT IT ALL DAY LONG?

Now arrange the circled letters to form the surprise answer, as suggested by the above cartoon.

Print answer here

I'M

PUZZLE 179

JUMBLE®

Unscramble these six Jumbles, one letter to each square, to form six ordinary words.

USUBED

MOARRY

LUFTAY

TEETIP

YORCUT

ABBIDE

WHAT THE COW WHO COULDN'T GIVE MILK CONSIDERED HERSELF.

Now arrange the circled letters to form the surprise answer, as suggested by the above cartoon.

Print answer here

AN “ ”

PUZZLE
180

JUMBLE®

Unscramble these six Jumbles, one letter to each square, to form six ordinary words.

CLITIA

DRIVEA

VARGEN

FROBEE

YAFFOP

INNOJE

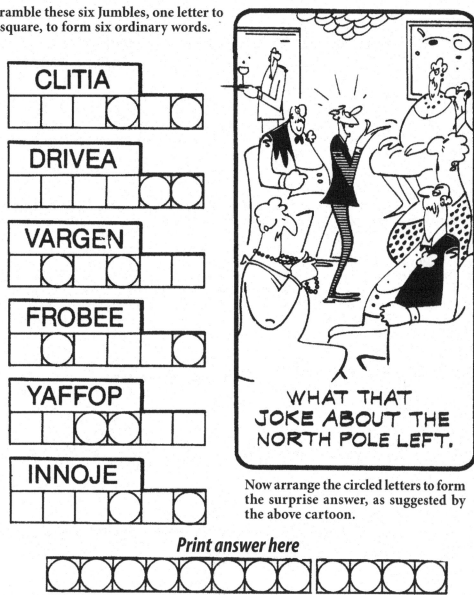

WHAT THAT JOKE ABOUT THE NORTH POLE LEFT.

Now arrange the circled letters to form the surprise answer, as suggested by the above cartoon.

Print answer here

ANSWERS

1. **Jumbles:** UPPER NOBLE FASTEN TROPHY
Answer: How to stop someone from talking in the back of the car—PUT HER IN THE FRONT

2. **Jumbles:** BURST MILKY IMPOSE ABUSED
Answer: You can prove your uprightness by taking this line —PLUMB

3. **Jumbles:** PAPER CABLE FACING ISLAND
Answer: It's not completely a "collapse"—just this— A "LAPSE"

4. **Jumbles:** PLUME FABLE HOOKED LOCATE
Answer: Comes under pressure when a driver steps on it— THE PEDAL

5. **Jumbles:** TWICE NOTCH RADISH SOOTHE
Answer: How far away did David stand from Goliath?— A STONE'S THROW

6. **Jumbles:** TRULY BAGGY ANSWER BESTOW
Answer: How those artillerymen were going—"GREAT GUNS"

7. **Jumbles:** ARRAY PIPER SECOND BUSHEL
Answer: What she said baking a good dessert was— EASY AS PIE

8. **Jumbles:** BANJO CYCLE THRASH DECEIT
Answer: What the man who invented the slide fastener hoped it would do—"CATCH ON"

9. **Jumbles:** NIECE LIBEL BROGUE HEARTH
Answer: Not the whole story of Lady Godiva—just this— A "BARE" OUTLINE

10. **Jumbles:** CROWN QUEST ADRIFT FLURRY
Answer: What tune makes a performer happy?— A "FOR-TUNE"

11. **Jumbles:** MERCY FEVER ZEALOT GAMBLE
Answer: What sailing a boat might be for an experienced sailor—A "BREEZE"

12. **Jumbles:** PHONY RUMMY AUTUMN FALLEN
Answer: On which he placed money of a certain amount— A MOUNT

13. **Jumbles:** LIMBO MADAM BLUISH MAGPIE
Answer: Where it could be said at a banquet—THE "DAIS"

14. **Jumbles:** SPURN POUCH MORTAR LAVISH
Answer: Could they be chiselers employed on "relief" projects?—SCULPTORS

15. **Jumbles:** ADAPT JEWEL BRUTAL MANIAC
Answer: There may be a fortune to be found at the bottom of this vessel—A TEACUP

16. **Jumbles:** EMPTY VISOR POLLEN FONDLY
Answer: What overeating makes the torso—"MORE SO"

17. **Jumbles:** HANDY BLOOM DETAIN UNWISE
Answer: How Jonah felt when the whale swallowed him— DOWN-IN-THE-MOUTH

18. **Jumbles:** SIEGE VIRUS TIPTOE DEBTOR
Answer: What some women claim to be—"DRESSTITUTE"

19. **Jumbles:** PERKY BISON UNEASY TACKLE
Answer: Looks at them coming and going—in both directions—SEES

20. **Jumbles:** OWING WHILE POPLAR MUSCLE
Answer: The general's favorite headquarters—HIS PILLOW

21. **Jumbles:** GOING FLUKE BEFALL CORRAL
Answer: What vampires often take a midnight— A COFFIN BREAK

22. **Jumbles:** VENOM CURRY PAUPER FELONY
Answer: How to make varnish disappear—REMOVE THE R

23. **Jumbles:** IDIOT WEDGE TERROR SLOUCH
Answer: What that famous author became after he passed away—A "GHOST" WRITER

24. **Jumbles:** SOUSE CLUCK ADJUST LOTION
Answer: What are your eyes for?—JUST FOR LOOKS

25. **Jumbles:** HEAVY MIRTH SHANTY MODERN
Answer: What happened to Lady Godiva's horse when he saw she had no clothes on?—IT MADE HIM "SHY"

26. **Jumbles:** POPPY ABHOR SHAKEN LAWYER
Answer: The hangman's favorite reading material— A "NOOSEPAPER"

27. **Jumbles:** RANCH IMPEL DEMISE TINGLE
Answer: What the ghost who joined the police force became—IN-"SPECTER"

28. **Jumbles:** FIFTY PANSY APPEAR PAROLE
Answer: What you might get from pirates—A "SEA TRIP"

29. **Jumbles:** MOUNT WAKEN ESTATE SOLACE
Answer: What the very busy doctor said to the invisible man—I CAN'T SEE YOU NOW

30. **Jumbles:** GLEAM JUDGE AMBUSH PAGODA
Answer: Why it was so hard to remove the cover from the marmalade jar—IT WAS "JAMMED"

31. **Jumbles:** FAITH SYLPH SAFARI TYPIST
Answer: Why the judge gave the man who stole some lingerie a suspended sentence—IT WAS HIS FIRST SLIP

32. **Jumbles:** ERUPT CAMEO CHERUB GAMBIT
Answer: A four-letter swear word often heard in legal circles—"OATH"

33. **Jumbles:** HYENA BASIC ADMIRE GENTRY
Answer: He felt like this after his laundry finally came back—A CHANGED MAN

34. **Jumbles:** POKER LIMIT UNLOCK CIPHER
Answer: What most people do when they meet that famous basketball star—LOOK UP TO HIM

35. **Jumbles:** VILLA PRUNE ENTIRE GRISLY
Answer: What bad sailors are called—PIRATES

36. **Jumbles:** CEASE OFTEN BESIDE TROUGH
Answer: You may get no rest from these singers—"TENORS"

37. **Jumbles:** TRILL DELVE APIECE MARLIN
Answer: Watches one's words—A LIP-READER

38. **Jumbles:** GAUDY IVORY PERMIT NICELY
Answer: He didn't know the meaning of fear until someone gave him this—A DICTIONARY

39. **Jumbles:** MAKER BASIS PUDDLE GOODLY
Answer: It's often eaten after dressing—SALAD

40. **Jumbles:** AVAIL SWOOP KINDLY ABSURD
Answer: To make a long story short there's nothing like having this—THE BOSS WALK IN

41. **Jumbles:** ABOUT STAID SMUDGE ENSIGN
Answer: How he survived the shipwreck— HE MISSED THE BOAT

42. **Jumbles:** DOGMA MOURN BUTTON ADROIT
Answer: Flowers may be appropriate when the romance is this—A "BUDDING" ROMANCE

43. **Jumbles:** CRESS AORTA POCKET FAMILY
Answer: What those things that hit the actors were— CAST AT THE CAST

44. **Jumbles:** PILOT CRUSH DAHLIA BEACON
Answer: A kind of scotch suitable for children—HOPSCOTCH

45. **Jumbles:** GORGE EXUDE NOZZLE FORBID
Answer: What the cop said to the burglar—FREEZE!

46. **Jumbles:** AMITY SHINY GUILTY TALKER
Answer: You wouldn't expect this to be a crooked poker hand, would you?—A "STRAIGHT"

47. Jumbles: GOUGE BALKY AVENUE SLEIGH
Answer: Liquid unfortunately much consumed on the road—GASOLINE

48. Jumbles: DEMON VISTA ADJOIN FAIRLY
Answer: Dive in! It can be heavenly—"DIVINE"

49. Jumbles: SMACK CRAZY PRIMED NOODLE
Answer: What happened when he accidentally pulled the altitude stick?—IT MADE HIM "SOAR"

50. Jumbles: EATEN BURST FABLED MUSTER
Answer: Who raided my vegetable patch?—"BEETS" ME

51. Jumbles: CROAK FOLIO EYELID KNIGHT
Answer: What a person who thinks by the yard and does by the inch might get—KICKED BY THE FOOT

52. Jumbles: FATAL ABBOT DETAIN BEATEN
Answer: How that busy executive followed his work schedule—TO A "TEE"

53. Jumbles: RAINY WELSH JUNIOR TACKLE
Answer: Never knows where his next car is coming from—A JAYWALKER

54. Jumbles: AWARD PRIZE GYRATE PONCHO
Answer: You can help keep those food bills down with this—A PAPERWEIGHT

55. Jumbles: CROWN BUILT FIDDLE PLOVER
Answer: What she gave him when he asked whether he could see her home—A PICTURE OF IT

56. Jumbles: LIBEL BASSO JOYOUS ATTAIN
Answer: All she knew about cooking was how to bring her husband this—TO A BOIL

57. Jumbles: TACKY FINNY ALWAYS FELLOW
Answer: Some gossips would rather listen to dirt than do this—CLEAN IT

58. Jumbles: MINER REARM HAZARD ABRUPT
Answer: People who sing like a canary seldom eat like this—A BIRD

59. Jumbles: MUSTY BRAWL EIGHTY GIGGLE
Answer: What they called those cigarette smugglers—"BUTT-LEGGERS"

60. Jumbles: VYING DUCHY HEALTH FAUCET
Answer: What those feline gossips were—"CATTY"

61. Jumbles: EXERT CASTE DEPUTY BOBBIN
Answer: When it comes to vacations, a girl can go to the mountains and see the scenery, or go to the beach and do this—BE THE SCENERY

62. Jumbles: CHIME SURLY ASYLUM GIBBET
Answer: What ignorance at the beach could be—"BLISS-TER"

63. Jumbles: LADLE KNAVE JACKET HIATUS
Answer: What a thoughtful wife has ready when her husband comes home from a fishing trip—A STEAK

64. Jumbles: LOWLY FINAL FEDORA EXTANT
Answer: When this happened, that comedian held his audience open-mouthed—THEY ALL YAWNED

65. Jumbles: DRAFT GRIME FINERY HAZING
Answer: A guy who claims he's always this must be all wet—RIGHT AS RAIN

66. Jumbles: LOUSE HOUSE BLEACH GROTTO
Answer: What a guy who's never at a loss for words often is—OUR LOSS

67. Jumbles: MILKY OZONE TOUCHY GOITER
Answer: What a husband misses when his wife isn't—HOME COOKING

68. Jumbles: WOVEN HABIT DECADE FAMISH
Answer: How the farmer knew it was time to get up—IT DAWNED ON HIM

69. Jumbles: SIEGE MAJOR NUANCE GARBLE
Answer: When a man brings his wife flowers for "no reason at all," there's usually this—A REASON

70. Jumbles: RUMMY FRAUD INFECT OBLONG
Answer: It's easy to stick to a diet these days if you just eat this—WHAT YOU CAN AFFORD

71. Jumbles: GULCH TIGER HERMIT PUNDIT
Answer: What the congressman always did when he finally got the floor—HIT THE CEILING

72. Jumbles: HUMAN LITHE MALLET NOGGIN
Answer: No matter how conditions improve in that big city, the subway always appears to be this—"IN A HOLE"

73. Jumbles: LANKY EXACT JERSEY IMPAIR
Answer: What the circus strong man turned crook had to be—A MAN OF "STEAL"

74. Jumbles: KNEEL CATCH ABOUND BOILED
Answer: How a barber usually likes to talk—BEHIND YOUR BACK

75. Jumbles: PUPIL GRAVE JOSTLE HEARTH
Answer: What those gossip reporters often give you the lowdown on—THE HIGHER-UPS

76. Jumbles: OUTDO ARRAY PUSHER BICKER
Answer: When you save money for a rainy day, someone always comes along at the last minute to do this—SOAK YOU

77. Jumbles: LAUGH SUITE BROOCH SIZZLE
Answer: He joined the fire department because she said this to him—GO TO BLAZES

78. Jumbles: LILAC ARMOR JINGLE IMBUED
Answer: What they call that man from whom many different girls get love letters—THE MAILMAN

79. Jumbles: CURIO BARGE NAPKIN MATURE
Answer: What some skaters might have to do in order to get better acquainted—BREAK THE ICE

80. Jumbles: SNARL DRAMA ACCESS HALVED
Answer: What the guy who was "all feet" when he danced was when they sat down—ALL HANDS

81. Jumbles: RODEO IDIOM CRABBY INJURY
Answer: He decided to watch his drinking—by only visiting bars that have this.—A MIRROR

82. Jumbles: LEAVE PRIOR SPONGE POORLY
Answer: If you think golf is only a rich man's game, look at these—ALL THE POOR PLAYERS

83. Jumbles: BLOOD YOUNG LAWYER VELVET
Answer: What his curly hair was beginning to do—WAVE GOOD-BYE

84. Jumbles: FANCY DAUNT ERMINE REDUCE
Answer: He got the job as a piano mover although he couldn't even do this—CARRY A TUNE

85. Jumbles: FRAME VISOR COUPON DRUDGE
Answer: He couldn't think straight because he always had this—CURVES ON HIS MIND

86. Jumbles: LIGHT PROVE INDUCE AMOEBA
Answer: Some people who don't pay taxes in due time—DO TIME

87. Jumbles: PEACE HASTY PARISH SPRUCE
Answer: What you might find in an automobile graveyard—HEAPS OF "HEAPS"

88. Jumbles: NOVEL PURGE MAINLY OBJECT
Answer: What the guard called the key to the jail, as he threw it away—THE CAN OPENER

89. Jumbles: TOOTH BOGUS INDUCT TRICKY
Answer: They drank to each other's health so often that this happened—BOTH GOT SICK

90. Jumbles: MINOR WAFER ABSORB MOSQUE
Answer: What briefs are usually "woven" from—"FIBERS"

91. Jumbles: VALVE MADAM WHENCE FLORID
Answer: Everybody was in debt but it's permitted—"ALL-OWED"

92. **Jumbles:** RUSTY CHANT FROSTY LAVISH
Answer: What it turned out to be when they forgot to hook on the dining car—A "FAST" TRAIN

93. **Jumbles:** DERBY GLORY HANDLE FACING
Answer: Sounds like a fisherman's dance—A REEL

94. **Jumbles:** OBESE DRYLY FROLIC IODINE
Answer: What the blushing bride was turning, whichever way one looked—REDDER

95. **Jumbles:** MAGIC VAGUE CRAFTY NAUSEA
Answer: What a person who loses his head would have difficulty doing—SAVING FACE

96. **Jumbles:** MERCY PHONY INBORN DEPICT
Answer: How the executioner would have preferred getting to work—BY CHOPPER

97. **Jumbles:** WHEAT ACRID MEMORY LAWFUL
Answer: What those Eskimos loved to do at dinnertime—CHEW THE FAT

98. **Jumbles:** POACH GROOM ORIGIN RADIUM
Answer: What some comedians make—DOUGH OUT OF CORN

99. **Jumbles:** BUSHY TOKEN MAKEUP ACHING
Answer: What it was for him when they repossessed the TV—A "SET BACK"

100. **Jumbles:** NOOSE ROACH POWDER TREATY
Answer: A mistake found in terrorism—"ERROR"

101. **Jumbles:** TARRY METAL HAUNCH INFORM
Answer: What a real firm makes that may go off in the heat—A "FIRE ALARM"

102. **Jumbles:** JUMBO COCOA MATRON LIZARD
Answer: Another name for Dracula—THE BLOOD COUNT

103. **Jumbles:** PIANO LUSTY MOSAIC CLERGY
Answer: Sounds like a dramatic last word—"CURTAIN"

104. **Jumbles:** HOBBY SOUSE AMBUSH INFANT
Answer: He has succeeded in business by being a man of great cultivation—OF HIS BOSS

105. **Jumbles:** LEAKY BLAZE CHUBBY POLICE
Answer: Using this, a golfer should keep the first part on the second—"EYE-BALL"

106. **Jumbles:** LOUSY TEASE MALICE HEIFER
Answer: What the potter's art consists of—"FEATS" OF CLAY

107. **Jumbles:** HAZEL CRAWL OFFSET MOHAIR
Answer: When you give the answers in "round" numbers, you're apt to come up with this—ALL ZEROS

108. **Jumbles:** MIRTH CRANK THRESH UNFAIR
Answer: His "position" in France gives him the right to vote—"FRANC-HIS-E"

109. **Jumbles:** MAUVE LIMIT LEEWAY WEASEL
Answer: Everything is "soaked" in the billfold—"W-ALL-ET"

110. **Jumbles:** PILOT GLOAT SWIVEL CHERUB
Answer: An insult that sometimes seems rather slight—A "SLIGHT"

111. **Jumbles:** PRUNE GUILD NEARBY MANIAC
Answer: What you might get when you overly indulge—A BULGE

112. **Jumbles:** CAPON TAWNY POLICY GRUBBY
Answer: Many people buy on time, but few do this—PAY THAT WAY

113. **Jumbles:** HEAVY FOYER LAGOON QUAINT
Answer: This sure made her face red!—ROUGE

114. **Jumbles:** ERUPT ROUSE CAUCUS JAILED
Answer: Take down for a customer—REDUCE THE PRICE

115. **Jumbles:** FORCE QUEEN EXODUS PIGEON
Answer: "I am the first one in the grammar class"—"PERSON"

116. **Jumbles:** SLANT GOOSE TYPIST SKEWER
Answer: What the anxiety-ridden soprano was evidently suffering from—"SONG-STRESS"

117. **Jumbles:** YEARN ONION STUDIO THEORY
Answer: What happened to the farmer's cattle?—NO ONE'S HERD

118. **Jumbles:** VALET BAGGY ARMORY CONVEX
Answer: How they acted at the undertakers' annual shindig—GRAVELY

119. **Jumbles:** COACH POKER STYLUS HEREBY
Answer: What you might have when two authors sue each other—A BOOK CASE

120. **Jumbles:** GLADE PARTY AGENCY NIMBLE
Answer: What a dentist might do about those missing teeth—"BRIDGE" THE GAP

121. **Jumbles:** BASIN DUSKY LARYNX PONDER
Answer: What the gardener said when the flowers wouldn't grow—"UPSY-DAISY"

122. **Jumbles:** TRILL BOUND GOVERN ROBBER
Answer: What the locksmith made when his shop caught fire—A BOLT FOR THE DOOR

123. **Jumbles:** PANSY CRAFT HUMBLE MEMBER
Answer: What did they engrave on the robot's tombstone?—RUST IN PEACE

124. **Jumbles:** NEEDY USURY COMMON RADISH
Answer: What she told her cowboy friend not to do—HORSE AROUND

125. **Jumbles:** BASIS LAPEL HAMMER ALBINO
Answer: Obligated according to law when you "concoct" A LIBEL—"LIABLE"

126. **Jumbles:** WAGON KINKY SOCIAL DOUBLE
Answer: What happened to the man who invented vanishing cream?—NOBODY KNOWS

127. **Jumbles:** FELON WAKEN MEADOW HORROR
Answer: Present at present but not present—"NOW-HERE" (nowhere)

128. **Jumbles:** HIKER FLOOD ENCAMP DELUXE
Answer: What she told her husband he had better do whole on that fishing trip—DROP A LINE

129. **Jumbles:** WALTZ UPPER KENNEL ANYWAY
Answer: When he saw the cops, the robber took off and left his accomplice to do this—TAKE THE "WRAP"

130. **Jumbles:** PERKY WEDGE ARCADE EMERGE
Answer: People who don't dye their hair could eventually do this—MAKE THE "GRAYED"

131. **Jumbles:** APPLY BURLY FAMILY JUNGLE
Answer: The kangaroo visited a shrink because he had been feeling this lately—JUMPY

132. **Jumbles:** FLUKE CAMEO SAFARI DRAGON
Answer: Frankenstein was lonely until he discovered how to do this—MAKE FRIENDS

133. **Jumbles:** BRIBE FLANK MODIFY ACTING
Answer: When they invented drip-dry clothes, this just about came to an end—THE IRON AGE

134. **Jumbles:** POWER BLOAT FACIAL CLOVER
Answer: What happened when he put dynamite into the refrigerator?—HE BLEW HIS COOL

135. **Jumbles:** KITTY LINEN CAMPER SALOON
Answer: What the ancient Romans could do easily that most moderns have difficulty doing—SPEAK LATIN

136. **Jumbles:** LIVEN FLUID INNING DEFAME
Answer: The dentist grew fat because almost everything he touched was this—FILLING

137. **Jumbles:** PATIO SCOUR ARCTIC IMPACT
Answer: "Haven't you ever seen this?"—"A COMIC STRIP"

138. **Jumbles:** DUNCE GAUDY INVERT BODILY
Answer: What did the bored cow say when she got up in the morning?—"JUST AN UDDER DAY"

139. **Jumbles:** ITCHY FLAKE DEFILE WALRUS
Answer: After another woman had "turned" his head, he obviously couldn't do this anymore—FACE HIS WIFE

140. Jumbles: GLEAM TYING PANTRY SCHEME
Answer: "How does a baby chick fit into its shell?"—"EGGSACTLY"

141. Jumbles: HYENA SPURN BUSILY POMADE
Answer: What do you get when you cross a cactus with a porcupine?—SORE HANDS

142. Jumbles: ALIVE CIVIL EITHER BALSAM
Answer: What do liars do after they die?—LIE STILL

143. Jumbles: AGENT BALKY INLAND BESIDE
Answer: What brings flowers?—THE "STALK"

144. Jumbles: SILKY PEONY MENACE SMUDGE
Answer: What should a sword swallower eat when he's on a diet?—PINS & NEEDLES

145. Jumbles: SWOON GRIMY ENTIRE MANAGE
Answer: Could be instrumental in a marriage—THE ORGANIST

146. Jumbles: STOKE ADULT BUCKLE EXCISE
Answer: What happened to the man who sued the porter?—HE LOST HIS CASE

147. Jumbles: GAUZE WHISK NOUGAT TAUGHT
Answer: What do you call it when pigs do their laundry?—HOGWASH

148. Jumbles: USURP OFTEN POCKET NOODLE
Answer: If you want to buy a good wig, you sure have this—TOUPEE FOR IT

149. Jumbles: ANKLE EMPTY BEHAVE DEAFEN
Answer: The patients didn't like that nurse because she was always trying to do this—NEEDLE THEM

150. Jumbles: ABOUT INKED BLOODY INHALE
Answer: What's wrong with eating this little ol' apple?—"O.K. I'LL BITE"

151. Jumbles: EXULT MOURN GUILTY PALACE
Answer: What tequila is—THE "GULP" OF MEXICO

152. Jumbles: AGATE PRONE CELERY HAPPEN
Answer: Why next year is a good year for kangaroos—IT'S "LEAP" YEAR

153. Jumbles: WIPED NATAL PLENTY ARTERY
Answer: What the big game was when they put their star mummy in as pinch hitter—ALL WRAPPED UP

154. Jumbles: ROBIN OPIUM GEYSER JANGLE
Answer: This was the grand way in which she proclaimed that she was a top model—"I'M-POSING"

155. Jumbles: AORTA GUILE STUPID HYMNAL
Answer: What kind of an experience was it when he looked into the mirror?—A SHATTERING ONE

156. Jumbles: TUNED PIETY RATION OMELET
Answer: What the ambassador's dog certainly was not—A "DIPLO-MUTT"

157. Jumbles: RANCH AGILE CLOUDY SINGLE
Answer: What goes up the stairs on its head?—A NAIL IN A SHOE

158. Jumbles: ALBUM FOIST HOPPER BOTTLE
Answers: How could she sing so high when she was this?—"SOLO" (so low)

159. Jumbles: QUIRE AGONY DEADLY ENGINE
Answer: What kind of an experience is it to travel by flying carpet?—A RUGGED ONE

160. Jumbles: BEGUN VOCAL EMPIRE MAYHEM
Answer: Could this beer be large?—"LAGER"

161. Jumbles: POLLEN MOBILE INBORN THORAX HAGGLE OMELET
Answer: A smart girl is supposed to know this—ALL THERE IS TO "NO"

162. Jumbles: FLABBY THRIVE MISLAY ENCAMP COOKIE ATTAIN
Answer: How they ate that fancy banana and ice cream dish—LICKETY-SPLIT

163. Jumbles: FEWEST MELODY OBLONG SHADOW PRAYER OUTWIT
Answer: What a ladies' lounge might be called—A "POWWOW-DER" ROOM

164. Jumbles: MISERY PILFER ASSURE WHENCE THIRTY STANZA
Answer: What an oldster sometimes prefers—A SIESTA TO A FIESTA

165. Jumbles: BARREN CROTCH FRACAS SHEKEL EMBODY DEBATE
Answer: How the rabbit managed to escape from the hunters—BY A "HARE'S" BREADTH

166. Jumbles: MILDEW JUSTLY FLEECE CORRAL SUBWAY ASYLUM
Answer: What graffiti are—SCRAWLS ON WALLS

167. Jumbles: AGENDA BLEACH FUSION WINTRY INNATE DAWNED
Answer: Why they were bored at the nudist camp—NOTHING WENT ON THERE

168. Jumbles: FOURTH ELDEST BOTANY JAGUAR GARISH IDONE
Answer: What a successful prize fighter usually has to consider—THE "RIGHTS" OF OTHERS

169. Jumbles: HORROR GADFLY FUTILE EXTENT PONCHO ABSORB
Answer: How some do-it-yourself freaks always seem to fix things—BEYOND REPAIR

170. Jumbles: UNPAID ORATOR WOEFUL NUDISM REDEEM JUGGLE
Answer: What a good photographer often has to know how to make—A "SNAP" JUDGMENT

171. Jumbles: CEMENT GOPHER DISARM PUZZLE FICKLE BANISH
Answer: An instant on the lips—A LIFETIME ON THE HIPS

172. Jumbles: CHARGE FALLOW GRUBBY ZODIAC ROSARY ANKLET
Answer: What kind of a character was the guy who was lying under a tree watching his wife mow the lawn?—A SHADY ONE

173. Jumbles: PRISON OUTLET WEASEL MOTIVE FROLIC CHUBBY
Answer: That shoe salesman has one woman who's his steady, and many this—OTHERS TO BOOT

174. Jumbles: APPALL NICETY MALADY HAPPEN PUMICE RITUAL
Answer: What the capital of that egotistical millionaire mostly was—CAPITAL "I"

175. Jumbles: CHERUB DABBLE IMMUNE MODIFY HUMBLE PULPIT
Answer: Where the school bus driver's problems were—ALL BEHIND HIM

176. Jumbles: BYWORD MOTIVE FORBID COMPLY SEPTIC PUSHER
Answer: What you might find at a haunted college—SOME SCHOOL "SPIRIT"

177. Jumbles: ASTHMA SLUICE HANSOM FECUND INVADE BEADLE
Answer: What a successful bookseller hopes to do—VOLUME BUSINESS

178. Jumbles: LEGUME JITNEY ALBINO KINDLY IGUANA TRAGIC
Answer: What did the tree say after the woodpecker pecked away at it all day long?—I'M GETTING BORED

179. Jumbles: SUBDUE ARMORY FAULTY PETITE OUTCRY BABIED
Answer: What the cow who couldn't give milk considered herself—AN "UDDER" FAILURE

180. Jumbles: ITALIC VARIED GRAVEN BEFORE PAYOFF ENJOIN
Answer: What that joke about the North Pole left—EVERYONE COLD

Need More Jumbles®?

Order any of these books through your bookseller or call Triumph Books toll-free at 800-335-5323.

Jumble® Books

More than 175 puzzles each!

Cowboy Jumble®
ISBN: 978-1-62937-355-3

Jammin' Jumble®
ISBN: 1-57243-844-4

Java Jumble®
ISBN: 978-1-60078-415-6

Jazzy Jumble®
ISBN: 978-1-57243-962-7

Jet Set Jumble®
ISBN: 978-1-60078-353-1

Joyful Jumble®
ISBN: 978-1-60078-079-0

Juke Joint Jumble®
ISBN: 978-1-60078-295-4

Jumble® Anniversary
ISBN: 987-1-62937-734-6

Jumble® at Work
ISBN: 1-57243-147-4

Jumble® Ballet
ISBN: 978-1-62937-616-5

Jumble® Birthday
ISBN: 978-1-62937-652-3

Jumble® Celebration
ISBN: 978-1-60078-134-6

Jumble® Circus
ISBN: 978-1-60078-739-3

Jumble® Cuisine
ISBN: 978-1-62937-735-3

Jumble® Drag Race
ISBN: 978-1-62937-483-3

Jumble® Ever After
ISBN: 978-1-62937-785-8

Jumble® Explorer
ISBN: 978-1-60078-854-3

Jumble® Explosion
ISBN: 978-1-60078-078-3

Jumble® Fever
ISBN: 1-57243-593-3

Jumble® Fiesta
ISBN: 1-57243-626-3

Jumble® Fun
ISBN: 1-57243-379-5

Jumble® Galaxy
ISBN: 978-1-60078-583-2

Jumble® Garden
ISBN: 978-1-62937-653-0

Jumble® Genius
ISBN: 1-57243-896-7

Jumble® Geography
ISBN: 978-1-62937-615-8

Jumble® Getaway
ISBN: 978-1-60078-547-4

Jumble® Gold
ISBN: 978-1-62937-354-6

Jumble® Grab Bag
ISBN: 1-57243-273-X

Jumble® Gymnastics
ISBN: 978-1-62937-306-5

Jumble® Jackpot
ISBN: 1-57243-897-5

Jumble® Jailbreak
ISBN: 978-1-62937-002-6

Jumble® Jambalaya
ISBN: 978-1-60078-294-7

Jumble® Jamboree
ISBN: 1-57243-696-4

Jumble® Jitterbug
ISBN: 978-1-60078-584-9

Jumble® Journey
ISBN: 978-1-62937-549-6

Jumble® Jubilation
ISBN: 978-1-62937-784-1

Jumble® Jubilee
ISBN: 1-57243-231-4

Jumble® Juggernaut
ISBN: 978-1-60078-026-4

Jumble® Junction
ISBN: 1-57243-380-9

Jumble® Jungle
ISBN: 978-1-57243-961-0

Jumble® Kingdom
ISBN: 978-1-62937-079-8

Jumble® Knockout
ISBN: 978-1-62937-078-1

Jumble® Madness
ISBN: 1-892049-24-4

Jumble® Magic
ISBN: 978-1-60078-795-9

Jumble® Marathon
ISBN: 978-1-60078-944-1

Jumble® Neighbor
ISBN: 978-1-62937-845-9

Jumble® Parachute
ISBN: 978-1-62937-548-9

Jumble® Safari
ISBN: 978-1-60078-675-4

Jumble® See & Search
ISBN: 1-57243-549-6

Jumble® See & Search 2
ISBN: 1-57243-734-0

Jumble® Sensation
ISBN: 978-1-60078-548-1

Jumble® Surprise
ISBN: 1-57243-320-5

Jumble® Symphony
ISBN: 978-1-62937-131-3

Jumble® Theater
ISBN: 978-1-62937-484-03

Jumble® University
ISBN: 978-1-62937-001-9

Jumble® Unleashed
ISBN: 978-1-62937-844-2

Jumble® Vacation
ISBN: 978-1-60078-796-6

Jumble® Wedding
ISBN: 978-1-62937-307-2

Jumble® Workout
ISBN: 978-1-60078-943-4

Jumpin' Jumble®
ISBN: 978-1-60078-027-1

Lunar Jumble®
ISBN: 978-1-60078-853-6

Monster Jumble®
ISBN: 978-1-62937-213-6

Mystic Jumble®
ISBN: 978-1-62937-130-6

Outer Space Jumble®
ISBN: 978-1-60078-416-3

Rainy Day Jumble®
ISBN: 978-1-60078-352-4

Ready, Set, Jumble®
ISBN: 978-1-60078-133-0

Rock 'n' Roll Jumble®
ISBN: 978-1-60078-674-7

Royal Jumble®
ISBN: 978-1-60078-738-6

Sports Jumble®
ISBN: 1-57243-113-X

Summer Fun Jumble®
ISBN: 1-57243-114-8

Touchdown Jumble®
ISBN: 978-1-62937-212-9

Travel Jumble®
ISBN: 1-57243-198-9

TV Jumble®
ISBN: 1-57243-461-9

Oversize Jumble® Books

More than 500 puzzles each!

Generous Jumble®
ISBN: 1-57243-385-X

Giant Jumble®
ISBN: 1-57243-349-3

Gigantic Jumble®
ISBN: 1-57243-426-0

Jumbo Jumble®
ISBN: 1-57243-314-0

The Very Best of Jumble® BrainBuste
ISBN: 1-57243-845-2

Jumble® Crosswords™

More than 175 puzzles each!

More Jumble® Crosswords™
ISBN: 1-57243-386-8

Jumble® Crosswords™ Jackpot
ISBN: 1-57243-615-8

Jumble® Crosswords™ Jamboree
ISBN: 1-57243-787-1

Jumble® BrainBusters™

More than 175 puzzles each!

Jumble® BrainBusters™
ISBN: 1-892049-28-7

Jumble® BrainBusters™ II
ISBN: 1-57243-424-4

Jumble® BrainBusters™ III
ISBN: 1-57243-463-5

Jumble® BrainBusters™ IV
ISBN: 1-57243-489-9

Jumble® BrainBusters™ 5
ISBN: 1-57243-548-8

Jumble® BrainBusters™ Bonanza
ISBN: 1-57243-616-6

Boggle™ BrainBusters™
ISBN: 1-57243-592-5

Boggle™ BrainBusters™ 2
ISBN: 1-57243-788-X

Jumble® BrainBusters™ Junior
ISBN: 1-892049-29-5

Jumble® BrainBusters™ Junior II
ISBN: 1-57243-425-2

Fun in the Sun with Jumble® BrainBusters™
ISBN: 1-57243-733-2